C000088625

RYDER CUP
PLAYER BY PLAYER

RYDER CUP
PLAYER BY PLAYER

First published in the UK in 2014

© G2 Entertainment Limited 2014

www.G2ent.co.uk

All rights reserved. No part of this work may be reproduced or utilised in any form or by any means, electronic or mechanical, including photocopying, recording or by any information storage and retrieval system, without prior written permission of the publisher.

Printed and bound in Europe

ISBN 978-1-782812-64-7

The views in this book are those of the author but they are general views only and readers are urged to consult the relevant and qualified specialist for individual advice in particular situations. G2 Entertainment Limited hereby exclude all liability to the extent permitted by law of any errors or omissions in this book and for any loss, damage or expense (whether direct or indirect) suffered by a third party relying on any information contained in this book.

All our best endeavours have been made to secure copyright clearance for every photograph used but in the event of any copyright owner being overlooked please address correspondence to G2 Entertainment Limited, Unit 9, Whiffens Farm, Clement Street, Hextable, Kent BR8 7PG

CONTENTS

Introduction

At the 2012 Ryder Cup in Chicago, which ended in the most dramatic fashion, one fact more than any other was apparent: this tournament is the finest that golf has to offer. A plethora of factors vindicate this. The sheer bedlam and emotion you see from the galleries, encapsulated in the massive roars that ring out around the course every time a significant putt is holed or fairway found. There's also the pervading feeling that this competition is of utmost importance, that it really matters to players and fans. And then you have the 'us versus them' factor – the difficult-to-quantify ingredient that establishes the Ryder Cup as rivals competing for supremacy, with both desperate for success.

It wasn't always this way, however. A sense of rivalry was barely apparent in the decades that led up to the groundbreaking decision in 1979 to include the rest of Europe in the mix. To appreciate the magnitude of this decision, you have to go back to the event's inception.

The Ryder Cup began in somewhat humble circumstances, the pipedream of a St. Albans' seed merchant. Following a Ryder Cup-style exhibition match at Gleneagles in 1921 between a team of American professionals and a side drawn from the British PGA, a second was scheduled for 1926 at Surrey's East Course at Wentworth.

Great Britain won both of these contests convincingly but, at the second match Samuel Ryder, having been captivated by some of the world's best players, decided to make the match official. Thus the Ryder Cup was founded and the first competition proper took place in 1927 at Worcester Country Club in Massachusetts, although Ryder himself was too ill to present the trophy he'd donated.

Early matches between the two sides were fairly even but, after the Second World War, the Americans began to dominate. They would go on to win 18 out of the following 22 events, occasionally punctuated by a courageous British performance (such as the legendary 'Concession' at Royal Birkdale in 1969).

It was so one-sided, in fact, that for some American players there was little point in playing as the event didn't showcase their skills. The 1973 Open

Above: *Samuel Ryder*

champion Tom Weiskopf, for instance, decided not to play at Royal Lytham & St Annes in 1977, taking the opportunity to go bear-hunting in Alaska instead. The antipathy of players such as Weiskopf typified a wider indifference, especially in America.

It was obvious that the one-sided nature of the event meant the Ryder Cup was losing its appeal. In fact, many

RYDER CUP PLAYER BY PLAYER

questioned whether the competition had a future. With humiliation heaped on humiliation and an absence of anything resembling a contest, the television companies had all but lost interest. Tough decisions had to be made…and quickly. The Ryder Cup had long since ceased to be a genuine contest.

The decision to include continental Europeans arose from a discussion in 1977 between Jack Nicklaus and the Earl of Derby, who was serving as the President of the Professional Golfers' Association. This radical measure was suggested by Nicklaus as a means to make the matches more competitive, to make the predictable nature of the event a thing of the past.

Unfortunately, decades of ugly, landslide defeats for the British team had left the side dispirited, the opposition indifferent and the future of the event hanging in the balance. Even when a desperate and despairing Professional Golf Association (PGA) widened its selection pool, first from Great Britain to Great Britain & Ireland and then to a Europe-wide team, it seemed, initially at least, to make little difference.

In the new European team's first outing at West Virginia's The Greenbrier

in 1979, they were hammered 17–11, and worse was to follow. Two years later, at Walton Heath, the Americans brought arguably the greatest Ryder Cup side ever assembled across the Atlantic and demolished them once again, 18½–9½.

The inescapable truth was that the decision to bring the Europeans into the fray hadn't had the immediate effect that Nicklaus et al desired. To stop the event from being put out of its misery, the European PGA needed to do something dramatic.

When the PGA asked one of Europe's most successful players, double major winner Tony Jacklin, to skipper the team for the 1983 tournament in Florida, there were just six months before it began. Moreover, there wasn't exactly a queue of candidates for the job. Jacklin would agree to the job, but only if a raft of assurances could be guaranteed, from team rooms and support staff to better clothing and new equipment, plus travel on Concorde for wives and the caddies. "I said, if I do it, it has got to be the way the Americans do it," Jacklin announced.

Thanks to Jacklin, the European team now looked – and felt – better than ever, and his positive approach didn't stop there: Jacklin's team selection suggested

Opposite: *Ryder presents the 1929 trophy to British captain George Duncan*

he meant business too. A revitalised Seve Ballesteros was back following his omission in 1981, and he was inspired by a stirring war-cry from his skipper. The Europeans weren't going to Palm Beach to make up the numbers; they were going with pride and belief.

This sense of determination filtered into the players' form in Florida. After the opening day, the visitors led for the first time on American soil. Both teams were level at 8-8 after the second day and, as the match progressed into the singles, an almighty battle ensued.

Ballesteros was involved in a thrilling contest with Fuzzy Zoeller and the Spaniard looked invincible at three-up with seven to play, but then his game wobbled alarmingly. He rallied at the 16th but still needed to win the final hole to take the match. Sitting in a bunker 240 yards from the pin, defeat seemed inevitable, but Ballesteros hit a three wood close to the green and got down in two to grab a remarkable half.

A miraculous pitch from Lanny Wadkins on the final hole against José Maria Cañizares gave the American a half, which ensured they retained the cup. When future captain Bernard Gallacher failed to get anything from

his singles match with Tom Watson, the hosts celebrated yet another victory but this time it was different. Defeat for Europe hurt, and not because it was another embarrassingly heavy loss – quite the opposite: it was agonisingly close and the Americans knew it. After decades of despair, the future looked promising.

Left: *The famous concession between Jack Nicklaus and Tony Jacklin at Royal Birkdale in 1969*

But could the next Ryder Cup on European soil build on this change in fortunes and see the home team prise the Holy Grail from American hands? The event took place at The Belfry and the European team boasted, among others, Masters champion Bernhard Langer and Open winner Sandy Lyle, as well as Ian Woosnam and Nick Faldo.

The Americans started well on the first day, claiming three of the four foursomes with Lanny Wadkins and Raymond Floyd impressing in two wins. But on the second day, the pendulum began to swing towards the Europeans. Seve Ballesteros was in defiant mood, claiming his first

Right: *Sam Torrance celebrates holing the winning putt in 1985*

RYDER CUP PLAYER BY PLAYER

two points playing alongside compatriot Manuel Piñero.

Europe seized the initiative, establishing a platform for their remarkable triumph. Craig Stadler and Curtis Strange – two-up with two to play against Bernhard Langer and Sandy Lyle – appeared certain to win their game.

Stadler, however, missed a three-foot putt on the last to hand their opponents an unlikely half, and with it the momentum in the match. Europe went into the final day leading 9-7 and full of confidence. In the end, it was down to Sam Torrance to secure the trophy, but the Scot was facing US Open champion Andy North and had fallen three holes behind.

Torrance fought back and it was neck-and-neck going to the 18th. After North's ball found water, Torrance made birdie with an 18-foot putt. The emotional Scot, who was in tears before the putt sank, raised his arms aloft to signal that the Ryder Cup, after 28 barren years, was finally in European hands. The grand alliance between Great Britain and the rest of the continent had at last been embraced.

The European team travelled to Muirfield Village in Ohio desperate to defend their title and prove their victory

at The Belfry was not a one-off. Tony Jacklin skippered Europe again and he was up against his old adversary Jack Nicklaus, rekindling the fond memories of their epic Ryder Cup tussle in 1969 – one of the rare occasions when the Great Britain team came close to winning.

That 1969 encounter, played at Royal Birkdale, ended in the Ryder Cup's first tie after perhaps the most sporting concession in golfing history. The final match saw Nicklaus level with Jacklin going up the final hole. The Golden Bear, playing in his first Ryder Cup, holed a five-foot putt to ensure America would retain the trophy.

However, rather than force Jacklin to hole a three-foot putt to halve their match, he conceded it, saying: "I don't think you would have missed that putt, but in these circumstances I would never give you the opportunity." The sporting world stood back in awe, all except US captain Sam Snead, who couldn't believe his star player had not made Jacklin putt.

At Muirfield Village 18 years later, events played out in similarly enthralling circumstances. The Europeans dominated the first two days' play and went into the final day's singles with a five-point lead. However, despite working their way into this commanding position, no one expected the final push to be easy and the Americans didn't waste time putting points on the scoreboard.

In the first match, mercurial Welsh wizard Ian Woosnam was one hole down going into the last against Andy Bean, but he could not summon up the birdie he needed for victory and the Americans were up and running. Then, Nick Faldo and José Maria Olazábal surprisingly lost against Mark Calcavecchia and Payne Stewart respectively and suddenly the tide was turning.

It was the increasingly tense game between Eamonn Darcy and Ben Crenshaw – which had exploded on the sixth green when Crenshaw, already two holes down, snapped his own putter in a fit of rage – that would help to settle the European team's nerves and send them on to victory.

Crenshaw – one of the game's greatest putters – had to complete his round putting with either a one iron or a sand wedge but, amazingly, he bounced back to all square going into the last. However, Darcy held his nerve and claimed an unlikely victory in his fourth Ryder Cup match.

And so it came down to the steely nerve of Bernhard Langer and the enigmatic brilliance of Seve to bring it home, with the safest of fours at the 17th from the Spaniard securing the cup for Europe. After a day of unbearable tension and excitement, they finally triumphed by 15 points to 13.

Following these back-to-back European victories, the hype preceding the next event at The Belfry was immense. It was another nail-biting affair that ended in stalemate for only the second time in the tournament's history.

America had it all to do going into the final day's singles and they fought back to win the first two matches. However, their momentum soon faltered. On the treacherous 18th, Payne Stewart sent his ball into the water to lose to Olazábal, and then he could only watch in horror as team-mate Mark Calcavecchia played exactly the same shot against Ronan Rafferty.

And then came the seminal moment that will always be synonymous with the 1989 event: Christy O'Connor Junior's famous two-iron to the 18th that saw him vanquish Fred Couples. Tears were flowing on the green and off.

In the end, it fell to José Maria Cañizares to get down in two on the 18th to win his match against Ken Green and ensure that Europe retained the trophy. However, defeats in the remaining four singles matches meant that Europe could not claim overall victory.

As the Ryder Cup entered the 1990s, events in the Gulf, where America and her allies were fighting to liberate Kuwait, set the tone for a tournament that would become known as the 'War on the Shore'. This was due to the behaviour of the highly charged American players led by Corey Pavin, who proudly wore a Desert Storm cap.

Bernard Gallacher had replaced Tony Jacklin as European captain and was confident of victory, but then again, so were the Americans. The fate of the cup was eventually decided on the last hole of the last match between Bernhard Langer and Hale Irwin. Langer, with the eyes of the world upon him, missed his six-foot putt for the half that would have given Europe a tie, and the Ryder Cup returned to America for the first time since 1983.

To quell any feelings of enmity between the sides, the Americans made the clever choice of the much-admired Tom Watson as their captain for the third consecutive event to be played at The Belfry. An amiable relationship between

Watson and Gallacher developed quickly and the first two days' play ended with just one point separating the teams. It was America who triumphed, however, as they stormed to six wins and two halves in the singles.

In 1995 at Oakland Hills, Gallacher skippered the Europeans for a third time and he was determined to get his hands on the trophy. After yet more dazzling golf and another nerve-jangling finish, the Europeans snatched a dramatic victory, the unlikely figure of Philip Walton sealing it with a win against Jay Haas. After decades of effortless American superiority, Europe had secured their second victory over the pond in six years. The trophy was heading back to Europe and it would stay there until 1999 after 1997's European victory at Valderrama. Skippered by the European team's most charismatic player, Seve Ballesteros, the home team amassed a commanding lead after the first two days, which proved just enough to withstand a last-day singles onslaught from the US team.

Going into the 1999 Ryder Cup at Brookline in Massachusetts, the home team, led by Ben Crenshaw, had grown sick of the taste of defeat. They wanted revenge and their determination to get their hands on the trophy was insatiable.

However, after the first two days the Europeans had raced into an impressive 10-6 lead. The Americans, fuelled by a pep talk from Texas governor and presidential candidate George W. Bush on the Saturday night, treated the final day like the Alamo.

Buoyed by a favourable draw and a raucous home crowd, the Americans won the first six matches of the day. Padraig Harrington pulled back a point for Europe, but the home team moved to within a half point of victory when Jim Furyk defeated Sergio García.

When Justin Leonard holed a 40-foot birdie on the 17th, he looked to have sealed the comeback. Leonard ran around punching the air and was swamped by caddies, team-mates and the players' wives. His opponent, José María Olazábal, who could still halve the hole with a birdie putt of his own, was left waiting on the green while the Americans celebrated presumed victory. When the pandemonium finally died down, the normally unflappable Spaniard struck his putt wide and the Americans continued their celebrations.

Their voracious march in clawing back point after point in the singles was worthy of the highest praise, but the Europeans and most of the watching world believed a line had been crossed. Sam Torrance branded the behaviour of the players and the whipped-up crowd 'disgusting', while Europe's captain, the normally placid Mark James, referred to it as a 'bear pit' in a book recounting the event

It was left to the patriotic yet calm head of Payne Stewart to put the event into perspective. "You have to understand," said Stewart in the aftermath of the unpalatable events of the Sunday afternoon, "that this is not life or death."

The distasteful end to proceedings had taken the shine off an incredible week's golf and one of the greatest comebacks in sporting history. The individual performances of the American team meant they fully deserved their triumph and the quality of their golf was at times utterly sublime.

However, for their performances as a team, the Europeans deserved more than they eventually got. Their achievement in running the opposition so close, despite being overwhelming underdogs and playing in the most hostile environment, shouldn't be underestimated.

It was clear that time was needed for players from both sides to reflect and move

Left: *The American players flood onto the green at Brookline in 1999*

on from events at Brookline. However, the next Ryder Cup, scheduled once more for The Belfry, was postponed due to the September 11th attacks. It was eventually played the following year at the original venue with the same teams that had been selected to play initially. The display boards at The Belfry still read 'The 2001 Ryder Cup'.

The sobering events of September 11th put the behaviour of the players and fans, not to mention the importance of the event, into stark context. It was clear that everyone involved in the Ryder Cup would not allow a repeat of the unsavoury atmosphere of Brookline, so, when the American team, captained by Curtis Strange, arrived in Warwickshire they were the model of respect and fair play.

After the first two days, the scores were tied at eight points each but, rather than take a cautious approach, Europe's captain, Sam Torrance, instead took a risk by sending his best players out first on the final day.

The gamble paid off handsomely.

Right: *Paul McGinley throws himself into the lake in triumph after Europe's 2002 victory at The Belfry*

Point followed point, with Seve's successor as European talisman, Colin Montgomerie, producing arguably the greatest performance of his professional career with a 5&4 hammering of Scott Hoch.

If Monty's win was the most impressive, then the biggest surprise came in the match between Welshman Phillip Price and world number two Phil Mickelson. Price's 25-foot putt on the 16th green sealed a memorable 3&2 victory and sparked jubilant celebrations. It was left to Paul McGinley to secure victory for Europe with a half against Jim Furyk. The Irishman celebrated by

throwing himself into the lake at the 18th draped in his home flag.

Sam Torrance, so dejected and drained three years earlier, this time cut an ecstatic yet humble figure. "It had nothing to do with me," said the emotional Scot. "I led the boys to water, and they drank copiously." After three long years

everyone had forgotten how good this competition could be.

Europe's comfortable 15½-12½ win was seen as a benchmark for what they could achieve, but many thought the winning margin would be difficult to emulate. However, events in 2004 at Oakland Hills confounded all expectations when Europe recorded their largest ever victory.

For many, the die was cast on the first day when the US captain Hal Sutton made the baffling decision to pair Tiger Woods and Phil Mickelson – hardly the best of friends – in the Friday four-balls and foursomes. The pair lost both their matches on the opening day as Europe surged into a 6½-1½ lead. By the end of the second day, the lead had been stretched to 11-5.

The Americans needed the spirit of Brookline in the final day's singles, but Europe's players kept their nerve and condemned their opponents to their biggest loss on home soil.

Sergio García disposed of Mickelson 3&2, while Lee Westwood defeated Kenny Perry 1 up. The stage was set for Colin Montgomerie, in only the sixth match out, to deliver the hammer blow against David Toms. It is a curious quirk of the Ryder Cup that in recent years the American side have invariably occupied higher positions in the world rankings but they tend to play as individuals, which explains their strong showing on the final day. The European team, by contrast, has been so much greater than the sum of its parts and shrewd captaincy – with the exception of Faldo in 2008, a man who played and presented himself in much the same way as the aloof Americans – allowed often inferior individuals to gel as a team and raise their game to a level unmatched by their opponents.

The 2006 and 2008 competitions saw comfortable wins for the home teams. First, a Darren Clarke-inspired Europe equalled their record-breaking winning margin on a highly emotional weekend at the K Club in Ireland. Captained by former Masters champion Ian Woosnam, the European team were imperious, none more so than Clarke, who had lost his wife Heather to cancer only the month before.

To have competed was one thing, to have dominated and won three points was another matter entirely. From the moment Clarke and his vanquished opponent Zach Johnson shook hands on the 16th hole to signal the Northern Irishman's victory, an emotional tidal wave rolled over the green. First to embrace Clarke was his caddie Billy Foster, followed by Tom Lehman, Ian Woosnam and then several players and caddies from both teams, as well as family and friends.

This incredibly emotional spectacle restored everyone's faith in the sport, and there was a feeling that the Ryder Cup had come full circle since 1999.

The 2008 competition held at Kentucky's Valhalla course saw Europe embarking on a quest to secure a fourth consecutive victory. However, it ended in a comfortable win for the Americans.

There was a minor undercurrent of animosity running through the weekend because the teams were captained by old rivals Paul Azinger and Nick Faldo. In Faldo (Europe's record points scorer and holder of the most appearances by any European), the away team were captained by someone whose insular nature made him one of the continent's greatest players but not one of its finest captains.

Europe had the better team and so for Faldo to guide them to defeat from such a position of strength was the mark of someone not cut out for leadership. Tony Jacklin he most certainly wasn't. In Paul Azinger, however, the Americans had the more astute and inspirational general, someone whose patriotic and outspoken nature helped lead his troops back to the promised land.

Faldo backloaded his team in the singles, sending out too many of his best players later on. With a better balance in his line-up, logic says Faldo would have cancelled out the 9-7 lead the US team took into the final day from the foursomes and four-balls, and then carved out a fourth consecutive European triumph. But it wasn't to be.

It was the younger players in the American side who caught the eye, especially the charismatic Boo Weekley and Anthony Kim. Their infectious nature and the 13th-man aspect of the local crowd carried the Americans over the line in a tournament to forget for the Europeans.

When play returned to Europe two years later, the venue was Wales's Celtic Manor and the home side was captained by Mr Ryder Cup himself, Colin Montgomerie. One of the greatest exponents of the matchplay art, this was the event he was born to lead. It was the first time the event had been held in Wales and there was a sense that the home side had learned their lessons from Faldo's 2008 ordeal.

Horrendous weather over the weekend saw play suspended twice, meaning the competition went into Monday for the first time in its history, but not before the weekend had thrown up some glorious play. Europe found themselves 4-6 down after the first two sessions, but they fought back in blistering fashion to go into the final day's singles with a three-point lead.

As Montgomerie stated after the competition, the trophy was not won on Monday, but on Sunday when Europe collected 5½ points out of six and every member of the 12-man team contributed. In the end, Europe only scraped over the line with 14½ points; half a point less and the Ryder Cup would have returned to America.

It was US Open champion Graeme McDowell who sealed victory against Hunter Mahan in a tense finish on the penultimate hole, unleashing a seething mass of human celebration on the 17th green. Victory had been bestowed on a captain once relentlessly ridiculed by the American galleries for his appearance and empty major trophy cabinet. For Montgomerie and Europe it had unfolded in such a unique and special way that it will live long in the minds of those who were there. Could this Welsh cliff-hanger ever be bettered? Few would have thought that possible, but how wrong they were. Everyone who followed the 2012 Ryder Cup at Chicago's Medinah Country Club could not fail to be united in the belief that this was one of the most unlikely and unexpected turnarounds that sport has yet produced.

Europe was captained by Seve's great friend and two-time Masters champion José María Olazábal, and the mood from the defending champions was upbeat. But, Ian Poulter aside, the team struggled over the first two days as the Americans, with Phil Mickelson and Keegan Bradley in outstanding form, raced into a commanding lead.

Going into the final day's singles, the European team trailed by 10 points to six and there was a palpable sense that the Americans would dispatch them without fuss on what had traditionally been their strongest day. But sometimes the presumption of victory can help to calm the nerves of the opposition and engineer an opportunity that can be grabbed with both hands. And this is precisely what the European team conspired to do with a dramatic 14½-13½ victory fuelled by an inspirational never-say-die spirit.

Every Ryder Cup throws up a hero or two, and this event was no different. For the third Ryder Cup in succession, Europe's talisman was Ian Poulter. Overwhelmingly self confident yet the epitome of patriotic pride, Poulter was unquestionably Ballesteros's representative on the course. "This Ryder Cup is not for the faint of heart," he proclaimed, and how right he was.

But Poulter's majestic four-point haul wasn't the only feat worthy of the highest praise. Step forward former Open champion Paul Lawrie, who thrashed an in-form Brad Snedeker 5&3, helped by arguably the shot of the week: a 40-foot chip in at the fourth hole.

And then there was Nicolas Colsaerts, who made a name for himself on the Friday when European heads were dropping courtesy of his laser-sighted putter, and Justin Rose. The point that Rose won against Phil Mickelson was unquestionably one of Europe's most pivotal.

Many times over the course of the 18 holes it looked like Rose was a beaten man but instead he sunk a succession of superb putts that gave the impression that Clark Kent had just walked onto the course.

Left: *The Ryder Cup*

On the final day, the Americans only needed 4½ points from the singles matches to regain the trophy but a front-loaded European side started strongly and had soon levelled the match. The final pairings saw the projected scores seesaw with nerve-shredding regularity as the combatants traded holes coming down the stretch. One moment America seemed assured of victory and the galleries reached fever pitch, the next, the Europeans had swung the balance in their favour and silenced the crowds. It was truly hide-behind-the-sofa-and-chew-your-nails stuff for the millions watching on TV.

However, the critical point was won by the ice-cool German Martin Kaymer. Kaymer, as opposed to Poulter, was an unlikely hero, coming off the back off a terrible six-month slump to beat Steve Stricker by draining a tough six-footer on the 18th. After countryman Bernhard Langer's agony at missing the crucial putt for the same prize 21 years earlier, the symmetry of this winning putt was impossible to escape.

The trophy was Europe's once more, the seventh victory in the last nine competitions. Seve would have been very proud.

Left: *Tiger Woods tees off at the 2012 Ryder Cup*

Alliss

It was perhaps inevitable that Peter Alliss would enjoy a successful career in golf. The son of Percy Alliss, one of Britain's finest players in the 1920s and 1930s, Alliss would go on to be regarded as not only one of the leading players of his day but also one of the game's most revered commentators.

After his father hired him to work as his unpaid assistant at Dorset's Ferndown Golf Club, allowing him time off during the week to compete in tournaments, Alliss decided to quit school at the age of 14 and pursue his dream of becoming as successful a golfer as his father.

He wasted no time in establishing himself among the top young players of the time. Just two years later, in 1947, aged only 16, Alliss turned professional and it wasn't long before he started playing tournaments on the British PGA circuit, the precursor to the European Tour.

Between 1954 and 1969, Alliss won 21 professional tournaments – including three British PGA championships – and was twice winner of the Vardon Trophy. In September 1958, he won the national championships of Italy, Spain and Portugal in three consecutive weeks. Alliss had five top-10 finishes in The Open Championship, coming closest in 1954 at Royal Birkdale when he finished just four shots behind the winner, Peter Thomson.

Alliss never managed to make his mark in America, however. Except for a brief six-week stint in 1954 and two appearances at The Masters, he never played on USPGA Tour. However, the impact Alliss made on the Ryder Cup is unequivocal.

He was first selected for the competition in 1953, and with the single exception of 1955, he represented Great Britain and Ireland in the event eight times, his last appearance coming in the famous halved match of 1969.

Playing in an era of American domination, Alliss compiled a respectable overall record, winning 10, losing 15 and halving just the one. He saved his best form for single competition and boasts a

5-4-3 record. His sole team victory came in the 1957 event, held in Yorkshire, when Britain, led by captain Dai Rees, beat the United States 7½ to 4 ½.

Alliss and his father can also boast to being one of only two father-and-son duos to have represented their country at this level: Antonio and Ignacio Garrido of Spain would later emulate them.

After his retirement as a player, Alliss would go on to be twice captain of the Professional Golfers' Association, and the first president of the European Women's Professional Golfers Association, as well as a successful writer and course designer.

However, it is for his television commentary that he would become most renowned. His first television work was for the BBC at the 1961 Open Championship, and by 1978, following the death of Henry Longhurst, he was its chief golf commentator. His mellifluous voice and iconic verbal dexterity, not to mention his in-depth knowledge of the game, cemented his legacy as one of the game's greatest commentators.

Above: Peter Alliss plays out of the rough

Name: Peter Alliss
Born: February 28th 1931, Berlin, Germany
Ryder Cups: 1953, 1957, 1959, 1961, 1963, 1965, 1967, 1969
Ryder Cup Wins: 1957, tie 1969
Major Wins: 0

Ballesteros

Severiano Ballesteros was born in Pedreña in 1957. Known simply as Seve, he played professional golf from 1974 to 2007 and was ranked world number one for much of the late-1980s. His achievements as an individual on the European tour – where he won 50 events – and as a player and captain of the Ryder Cup team cannot be overstated.

The sport ran through his family – his uncle and older brother were also professional golfers – so Ballesteros started playing on the beaches near his home with a 3-iron when he was only seven. He soon honed his skill on local courses and turned professional at 16. The flamboyant, sometimes wayward but invariably brilliant golfer made a mark on the international scene by coming second in The Open Championship just two years later, a year in which he also won the European Tour Order of Merit for the first time. He went on to win the accolade for the following two years, and six times in total.

In 1979 he won his first major (The Open), although he had to make an unlikely 70 on the final round to secure victory. Despite hitting into the car park on the 16th, he still made birdie and kept himself in the hunt. The win ushered in a decade when he played with a mixture of intoxicating brilliance and childish belligerence (mostly the former), which saw him claim another four major titles. His reaction after holing the putt to secure the 1984 Open at St Andrews remains one of sport's iconic moments, and his final round 65 to win his last major at Royal Lytham in 1988 was perhaps the finest round of golf ever played.

This was also the period when he came to embody the spirit of the Ryder Cup. He scored 22½ points from 37 matches overall, and his pairing with compatriot José María Olazábal, which yielded 11 wins and two halves from just 15 matches, was the most successful in the cup's history. The pinnacle of Seve's achievements in the tournament surely came on home soil at Valderrama in 1997, however, when he captained the side to victory despite a strong American comeback on the final day.

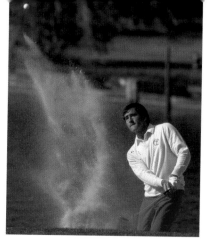

Left: *Seve plays out of a bunker*

He struggled with back injuries throughout the 1990s and eventually retired in 2007 to design golf courses. In 2008, Seve was diagnosed with a cancerous brain tumour and underwent surgery and chemotherapy. With his condition deteriorating, he was awarded his second Lifetime Achievement Award at the 2009 BBC Sports Personality of the Year Awards. It was another evening charged with emotion and there was barely a dry eye in the house as Olazábal presented him with the trophy. When Seve died aged just 54 in 2011 sport globally lost one of its greatest talents and finest ambassadors.

The following year, the European Ryder Cup team under Olazábal staged one of the greatest comebacks in sporting history to reclaim the trophy. The Europeans were four points down going into the last-day singles, traditionally the preserve of the Americans. But Ian Poulter, Justin Rose and Martin Kaymer somehow turned the tables to give Europe the unlikeliest of victories. Such was the outpouring of emotion on the course that most of the European players were reduced to tears. The man who had become synonymous with the event and who had inspired his team to victory several times from seemingly impossible situations would surely have allowed himself a satisfied smile.

Name: Severiano Ballesteros Sota
Born: April 9th 1957, Cantabria, Spain
Died: May 7th 2011, Cantabria
Ryder Cups: 1979, 1983, 1985, 1987, 1989, 1991, 1993, 1995
Ryder Cup Wins: 1985, 1987, tie 1989, 1995 and 1997 (as non-playing captain)
Major Wins: 5 (U.S. Masters 1980, 1983; The Open Championship 1979, 1984, 1988)

Barnes

Taught how to play by his father and later a pupil (and future son-in-law) of the great Max Faulkner, the 1951 Open champion, Brian Barnes turned professional in 1964 and went on to become one of the leading European Tour golfers of the 1970s.

Barnes finished in the top eight of the Order of Merit every year from 1971 to 1980 and won nine events on the tour between 1972 and 1981. He also boasted three top-10 finishes at The Open Championship, the best of which saw him tie for fifth in 1972.

However, it was in the Ryder Cup that Barnes arguably shone brightest. He played for Great Britain & Ireland, and finally Europe, in six consecutive Ryder Cups, beginning with the tied match at Birkdale in 1969, the scene of Jack Nicklaus's remarkable concession to Tony Jacklin.

Barnes's Ryder Cup story lasted until 1979. En route to his final chapter he had established a successful partnership with Bernard Gallacher in foursome and four-ball matches. However, he is perhaps best remembered for achieving the remarkable feat of beating the formidable Jack Nicklaus twice in one day in Pennsylvania in 1975.

A desperate opening session for the visitors had ended with America cruising to victory in all four of the foursome matches. This meant that the match was as good as finished and all that was left for Britain & Ireland was to try to regain their pride, and no one showed their mettle more than Barnes. His showdown with Nicklaus looked like a foregone conclusion.

The Golden Bear had just won his fourth PGA Championship and came into the Ryder Cup bubbling with confidence. However, first blood on the final morning went to Barnes with a 4&2 victory. Nicklaus was desperate for revenge and his request to captain Arnold Palmer for a rematch in the afternoon was received positively.

On the first tee Nicklaus confidently told his partner: "There ain't no way you're going to beat me again." But,

despite a fine start with two birdies, it was Barnes who strolled to a 2&1 victory.

His overall Ryder Cup record saw him win 10 matches, lose 14 and tie just the once. His singles record saw him notch up five wins and five losses.

Name: Brian Barnes
Born: June 3rd 1945, Surrey, England
Ryder Cups: 1969, 1971, 1973, 1975, 1977, 1979
Ryder Cup Wins: 0, tie 1969
Major Wins: 0

Clarke

To many, Darren Clarke is the talented bon viveur with the build of an Ulster farmer, whose majestic 2011 Open victory finally silenced those who thought his fun-loving tendencies off the course tended to obscure his golfing gifts.

Yet ultimately, it for his incredible bravery in playing, let alone performing superbly, in the 2006 Ryder Cup, just six weeks after his wife Heather's untimely death that the mighty Ulsterman will forever be remembered.

Clarke had turned professional 16 years prior to his emotionally charged performances at Ireland's K Club, making steady progress in his early years on the European Tour. In October 1993, Clarke won his maiden tour event at the Alfred Dunhill Open in Belgium, and as the years passed he continued to rack up professional titles.

His worldwide breakthrough came in 2000 when he won his first World Golf Championship event, defeating Tiger Woods in the final at the WGC-Andersen Consulting Match Play Championship.

In 2002, he became the first player to win the English Open three times, and the following year he became the first player other than Tiger Woods to capture more than one World Golf Championship. However, a major triumph continued to elude him until, finally, in 2011 he climbed his personal Everest and won the 140th Open Championship at Royal St George's in Kent by three shots from Phil Mickelson and Dustin Johnson. His winning margin told its own story. Clarke could easily have cracked under pressure, but he held his nerve on the final day to secure an emotional victory.

Clarke's Ryder Cup record is equally impressive. He won 10 and drew three of his 20 matches, and his partnership with Lee Westwood was one of the most successful of the modern era. He had played an integral part in three victories for Europe prior to 2006 – first in 1997 at Valderrama, and again in 2002 and 2004. The defeat in ignominious circumstances in Brookline in 1999 was his only loss.

However, as 2006's event approached, Clarke, a wild card pick by captain Ian Woosnam, wasn't sure he would be able to perform and would only be a burden on his team-mates. But he decided he wanted to play, and as he stepped on to the first tee on the opening day, the roar of support could be heard all over Ireland.

Clarke composed himself and thundered his drive down the centre of the fairway, somehow producing a birdie on the first hole. Five hours later, Clarke and his partner Westwood had seen off Phil Mickelson and Chris DiMarco and their remarkable win ensured Europe got off to a sound start.

Woosnam wisely rested Clarke in the afternoon, but the next morning there was further joy when, playing again with Westwood, Clarke chipped in at the 16th to see off Jim Furyk and Tiger Woods.

Woods, who had lost his father earlier in the year, embraced his good friend.

And it was on the same green, in the singles, where Clarke defeated the soon-to-be Masters champion Zach Johnson. Clarke raised his arms and, with tears running down his cheeks, looked skywards. His three points from three had helped Europe to a resounding victory, and the golfing world stood as one to applaud his fortitude.

Name: Darren Christopher Clarke
Born: August 14th 1968, Dungannon, Northern Ireland
Ryder Cups: 1997, 1999, 2002, 2004, 2006
Ryder Cup Wins: 1997, 2002, 2004, 2006
Major Wins: 1 (The Open Championship 2011)

Coles

Neil Coles may not have become one of the game's superstars – indeed he never won a major – but for consistency and longevity his career ranks alongside the best. He withdrew from the Masters in 1966 and never played in either of the other American majors due to a fear of flying, but his record at The Open Championship was impressive: in 1961 he finished third at Royal Birkdale behind Arnold Palmer and Dai Rees, a second-round 77 denying him the claret jug; and in 1970 at St. Andrews he led after the first day and was only three behind Lee Trevino before the final round. Trevino faltered so Coles had a chance to pounce, but a 76 allowed Jack Nicklaus to steal the win.

In 1973 at Troon he was eight shots off the pace after the second round and still seven behind Tom Weiskopf going into the final round, but a magnificent 66 saw him pressure the American down the stretch. Unfortunately, Coles ran out of holes and came up a few strokes short.

He played himself into contention again at Carnoustie two years later. He was five shots off the pace after the second round but then shot a 67 to close the gap to South African Bobby Cole. Cole then had a poor final round of 76 but Coles also faded and handed victory to Tom Watson by three shots.

For a man who made it as high as seventh in the world rankings and had 45 professional wins, his Ryder Cup record is unremarkable, although the British team was considerably inferior to the American for most of his career. He only managed a win and a half in 1961 but came away from the 1963 event at the Atlanta Athletic Club with a creditable point even though the Europeans were humiliated 23-9. He scored two points at Royal Birkdale in 1965 and another brace over Doug Sanders in the singles at the Champions Club two years later. The highlight of his Ryder Cup career came in the famous tied match at Royal Birkdale in 1969 when he secured 2½ points.

Above: *Neil Coles at the 1970 Open Championship*

Thereafter, American dominance ensured that barely anyone from the Great Britain & Ireland team secured more points than they lost.

At the age of 67 he became the oldest man to win a senior event, and he also became only the second man (after Sam Snead) to win a professional event in six different decades. He was inducted into the World Golf Hall of Fame in 2000 and was chairman of the European Tour's board of directors until 2013.

Name: Neil Chapman Coles
Born: September 26th 1934, London, England
Ryder Cups: 1961, 1963, 1965, 1967, 1969, 1971, 1973, 1977
Ryder Cup Wins: tie 1969
Major Wins: 0

Donald

Luke Donald played at Hazlemere and Beaconsfield Golf Clubs before applying for a scholarship to the Northwestern University in the U.S. In winning the NCAA Division Men's Golf Championships in 1999 at the age of 22, he beat the record set by Tiger Woods. He turned professional in 2001 and earned more than a million dollars in his debut season.

In 2004 he was on scintillating form and won both the Omega Masters and Scandinavian Masters. He accumulated enough points to make the Ryder Cup squad and then scored 2½ in the competition itself as Europe routed the Americans 18½-9½ at Oakland Hills. He then banked another three points as Europe demolished the U.S. by the same score at the K Club two years later.

The 2010 Ryder Cup was plagued by bad weather – which led to a revision in the format but not the points on offer – and Donald again notched three vital points as Europe edged home by a single point on the Monday. In 2012 he played a crucial part in the epic fight-back from the Europeans, although it wasn't until Saturday's morning foursomes that he scored a point. He managed another with Sergio García in the afternoon four-balls but Europe were still trailing 10-6 going into the singles on Sunday. Donald led the team out with a narrow victory over Bubba Watson. The European team drew inspiration from first Donald and then Poulter, McIlroy, Rose and Lawrie as the front-loaded team blew the American big guns out of the water.

Donald now has 15 tournament wins, with five on the PGA Tour and seven on the European Tour. His best results in the majors have been third at the 2005 Masters and the 2006 PGA, eighth at the 2013 U.S. Open, and fifth at the 2009 and 2012 Open Championships. However, he has won the European Masters, the Scandinavian Masters, the WGC World Cup, the Honda Classic and the Madrid Masters. His biggest individual win came at the 2011 WGC Accenture Match Play Championship

Above: *Luke Donald of England selects a club*

where he dethroned then world number one Martin Kaymer.

Later in the year he won the prestigious BMW PGA Championship at Wentworth, following this up with victory in the rain-affected Scottish Open. He duly found himself at the top of the world rankings, a position he held for 40 weeks until Rory McIlroy overtook him 2012. The pair then traded the top spot for most of the next year before Tiger Woods's return to form.

Above: *Luke Donald of England selects a club*

Name: Luke Campbell Donald
Born: December 7th 1977, Hertfordshire, England
Ryder Cups: 2004, 2006, 2010, 2012
Ryder Cup Wins: 2004, 2006, 2010, 2012
Major Wins: 0

Faldo

Nick Faldo was the most professional British golfer in terms of attitude, commitment and sheer bloody-mindedness for nearly a generation, certainly since Tony Jacklin. Despite being labelled 'Foldo' by the press after a number of high-profile failures at the major championships in his early career, he refused to buckle and spent the mid-1980s refining his technique. He went on to win six major titles and was ranked as the world number one for 98 weeks in the 1990s.

Inspired by Jack Nicklaus, Faldo started playing as a teenager. While working as a carpet fitter in 1975, he then won the British Youths and the English Amateur Championships. He turned professional the following year and soon made an impact when he became the youngest man to play in the Ryder Cup, albeit in a losing cause during a period of American dominance. As Faldo perfected his swing and developed into the finest golfer of his generation, he dragged an ailing British and then European team into a different era. He came third in the 1978 European Tour Order of Merit and eventually topped the list in 1983.

The American team was about to run into a European side at its best at The Belfry. The opposition had every right to be confident as they hadn't lost the trophy since 1957 and they duly started well in 1985. But the Europeans pulled the score back from 1-3 to 6-6 and they then led 9-7 going into the singles. Faldo may have lost his match but Europe dominated what was usually their weakest day and they won 16½-11½.

Two years later Faldo scored 3½ points as Europe won again. He then won his first Open Championship at Muirfield. In 1989 he was again the form man in the European team but he couldn't secure a half against Lanny Wadkins in the singles that would have won the trophy outright. Instead, Europe retained it after a tie. Faldo's vital points at Oak Hill in 1995 ensured the trophy returned to Europe, and he again proved his mettle in the emotional win at Valderrama two years later.

Sadly Faldo's captaincy didn't live up to his playing. In 2008 he led a European team that looked much stronger on paper than their counterparts to a five-point defeat. He unwisely back-loaded the singles and sent too many good players out late rather than trying to wrest the initiative from an American team that led 9-7.

Faldo amassed 40 career wins, with 30 coming on the European Tour. He was inducted into the World Golf Hall of Fame in 1997 and was made a Member of the Order of the British Empire in 1998. In 2006 he became the primary golf analyst for CBS Sports.

Name: Sir Nicholas Alexander Faldo
Born: July 18th 1957, Hertfordshire, England
Ryder Cups: 1977, 1979, 1981, 1983, 1985, 1987, 1989, 1991, 1993, 1995, 1997, 2008 (as non-playing captain)
Ryder Cup Wins: 1985, 1987, tie 1989, 1995, 1997
Major Wins: 6 (U.S. Masters 1989, 1990, 1996; Open Championship 1987, 1990, 1992)

Gallacher

Bernard Gallacher sums up what it was like to be a professional European golfer at a time of complete American dominance in the Ryder Cup. But, like his countryman Robert the Bruce, he tried and tried until he finally tasted the success that he'd worked towards for more than a quarter of a century. He embodies that un-quantifiable spirit and is living proof that a team can be so much more than the sum of its parts.

Gallacher took up the sport aged 11 and won the Lothians Boys Championship in 1965. Two years later he'd developed sufficiently to win the Scottish Amateur Stroke Play Championship so he immediately turned professional. He won the Rookie of the Year Award in 1968 and then won his first four professional tournaments in Zambia and Europe (the tour itself wouldn't be founded until 1972).

In 1969 at the age of just 20 he became the youngest man to be selected for the Great Britain team in the Ryder Cup. Thanks to Jack Nicklaus's wonderful sportsmanship on the 18th at Royal Birkdale, Tony Jacklin secured a half and the match was tied. (Jacklin had won that year's Open Championship and was Britain's great golfing hope. This was in Nicklaus's mind when he conceded the putt as he didn't want his friend to miss and put the brakes on a burgeoning career.)

Thereafter, American dominance was unwavering and first British (and Ireland) and then European teams were summarily dispatched. The tide began to turn in the early 1980s but Gallacher was past his best come the 1985 tournament and wasn't selected. How he must have rued the chance to beat the Americans at The Belfry but his time would eventually come.

As captain in 1991 he led the Europeans to the brink of victory at Kiawah Island but the Americans won by a point after going into Sunday's singles level. In 1993 Gallacher was again at the helm but, despite leading after Saturday afternoon's four-balls, his team again faded to lose by

a couple of points after the singles.

At Oak Hill in 1995, Gallacher finally delivered a victory that no one in the golfing fraternity could begrudge him. Friday morning's foursomes finished level at 2-2 but the Americans seized the advantage in the afternoon four-ball, with only David Gilford and Seve Ballesteros salvaging a point for the Europeans.

On Saturday morning first Faldo and Montgomerie and then Torrance and Rocca blew the Americans away and the match was square going into the afternoon's four-ball. This time the American pairings dominated and only Woosnam and Rocca prevented a whitewash. The Americans were traditionally strong on Sundays and a tough ask became a mountain when Seve was trounced 4&3 by Tom Lehman in the opening match. But the Europeans then hit their straps as Clark, James, Monty, Faldo et al clawed back the deficit. With fingernails chewed to the quick, it was left to the virtually unknown rookie Philip Walton to secure victory at the last when

he beat Jay Haas.

Gallacher needed his fighting spirit once again when, in 2013, he suffered cardiac arrest during a function at Banchory Golf Club. If the hotel hadn't had a defibrillator he wouldn't have survived, and his general fitness kept him alive when he suffered further arrests on the way to hospital. Three months later, he was back on the golf course, another miracle recovery complete.

Name: Bernard Gallacher
Born: February 9th 1949, Bathgate, Scotland
Ryder Cups: 1969, 1971, 1973, 1975, 1977, 1979, 1981, 1983, as non-playing captain: 1991, 1993, 1995
Ryder Cup Wins: 1995 (as non-playing captain)
Major Wins: 0

Above: *Bernard Gallacher with the Ryder Cup*

García

With his father Victor the professional at his home club, El Nino started playing golf at the age of three and had become club champion by the age of 12. Four years later, he set a record as the youngest player to make the cut at a European Tour event, the 1995 Turespaña Open Mediterranea.

Inspired by the heroics of Seve Ballesteros and under the watchful eye of his father, García continued to show prowess and turned professional in 1999, shortly after shooting the lowest amateur score in that year's Masters.

His first title on the European Tour came the same year at the Irish Open, in only his sixth start as a professional. However, it was later that year, with his second-place finish at the PGA Championship, that he achieved worldwide prominence.

García's gripping duel with eventual winner Tiger Woods will always be remembered for his iconic six-iron on the 16th. With his ball up against a tree trunk in the rough, and the green hidden from view, García swung with all his might, his eyes clasped shut, and hit a low curving fade that ran up onto the green. As the ball arrowed onto the dance-floor, the Spaniard sprinted back onto the fairway and then leaped into the air to see the result.

Within weeks, he had also become the youngest player to compete in the Ryder Cup. Like his hero Seve, García was immediately captivated by the event, despite the disappointment of Europe's defeat in Brookline.

García won his first PGA Tour event at the 2001 MasterCard Colonial in Texas, making him the youngest tour winner since 20-year-old Tiger Woods in 1996. García won again at the Buick Classic in New York the same year, and he kept his good form going into 2002 with victory in the Mercedes Championships.

The PGA wins kept coming, including a second Buick Classic in 2004, but a major triumph would continue to elude him. He came close to winning the 2007 Open Championship, losing a four-

Left: *Sergio García after winning the 2008 Players Championship*

hole playoff to Pádraig Harrington by one stroke.

The following year, Harrington got the better of his Ryder Cup teammate once more, this time in the PGA Championship. However, 2008 wasn't a complete disappointment for García as he notched an impressive PGA win early in the year at the revered Players Championship, plus securing a career-high third place in the Official World Golf Rankings.

García is seen less as a major winner in waiting and more the heir to Colin Montgomerie's throne: European great and Ryder Cup icon.

His performances in his six appearances thus far suggest that he is more at home with a team dynamic than under the pressures of solo battle. García's singles record is patchy: four defeats and two wins, although his victory over Phil Mickelson in 2004 gave Europe the momentum it needed to vanquish the Americans at Oakland Hills.

Yet when sharing the responsibility with a partner, García's performances are second to none: an excellent record in the four-balls, six wins and three halves outweighing two defeats, and a return in the foursomes that is nothing short of sensational: eight wins from 11.

García has proved to be one of Europe's most influential Ryder Cup performers, playing a significant role in the continent's memorable recent successes. Whatever happens in his major and individual future, his place in Ryder Cup lore is undoubtedly assured.

Name: Sergio García Fernández
Born: January 9th 1980, Castellon, Spain
Ryder Cups: 1999, 2002, 2004, 2006, 2008, 2012
Ryder Cup Wins: 2002, 2004, 2006, 2012
Major Wins: 0

Jacklin

No superlative is too great for the two-time major winner who breathed new life into the Ryder Cup and made it what it is today. Easily the best British golfer of his generation, it is as both a player and captain that Tony Jacklin's name is synonymous with everything that the Ryder Cup stands for.

The incredible feat that Jacklin managed to pull off as captain in his four Ryder Cup matches in the eighties was to blend together and inspire the continent's supremely talented individuals into extraordinarily effective team performances.

From a showpiece event that the USA were always expected to walk, he helped transform the Ryder Cup into one of the most tightly contested and hotly anticipated battles across any sport

However, with a playing record of 13 wins, 14 losses and eight halves during a period of U.S. dominance, Jacklin had already made his mark. After making his debut in 1967, Jacklin was the newly crowned Open champion when he arrived to play in the 1969 match at Royal Birkdale. It was here that he became a key figure in the event's most endearing moment.

In the final singles head to head on the course, in what had been an extremely mean-spirited match to this point, Jacklin holed an incredible 50-foot eagle putt on the 17th to remain alive in his match against Jack Nicklaus. With the scores level at 15½ points each, Nicklaus and Jacklin, went down the final hole all square.

The Golden Bear's par meant the United States would escape with at least a draw and retain the trophy no matter what. But with his captain, Sam Snead, on the sidelines itching for the outright win, Nicklaus picked up his opponent's marker and conceded Jacklin's tricky putt.

The match was halved and the 1969 Ryder Cup was drawn. "I don't think you would have missed that, Tony," Nicklaus said, "but I didn't want to give

you the chance." His team, especially captain Sam Snead, were furious, but the world continues to applaud the gesture to this day.

The following year Jacklin won his second major title, the U.S. Open, by seven strokes on a windblown Hazeltine National Golf Club course. His was the only victory in the U.S. Open by a European player in an 84-year span until Northern Ireland's Graeme McDowell ended that streak in 2010.

Jacklin went on to play in five Ryder Cups, including the first time continental Europe was represented in 1979. However, by then, the event was on its knees, viewed as nothing more than a victory procession for the Americans.

Yet, this was all to change when Jacklin captained the team for the first time in 1983, where his opposing number was none other than Jack Nicklaus. What followed was a narrow one-point defeat and a gallant attempt to wrest back the Ryder Cup for the first time since 1969.

Despite losing, Jacklin's side had

Right: *Tony Jacklin in action*

proved that the event was far from a one-sided affair any more. They only needed to take the final step and the Americans would no longer see the game as a foregone conclusion. He didn't have to wait long.

By restoring pride in the locker room and professionalising the European approach to the event, he led his side to a landmark victory in 1985 at The Belfry, their first for 28 years. In 1987, his European team went one step further, achieving something that had never been done previously by beating the Americans on their own soil at Ohio's Muirfield Village.

The tied match at the Belfry in 1989 – in which Europe retained the trophy – was Jacklin's final match as captain. He knew it was time to pass the baton to let his Ryder Cup revolution continue. What Jacklin orchestrated was, quite simply, one of the greatest turnarounds the game has ever seen, and it is no exaggeration to say that without him the Ryder Cup as we know it wouldn't exist.

Name: Anthony Jacklin
Born: July 7th 1944, Lincolnshire, England
Ryder Cups: 1967, 1969, 1971, 1973, 1975, 1977 and as non-playing captain: 1983, 1985, 1987, 1989
Ryder Cup Wins: tie 1969, and as non-playing captain: 1985, 1987, tie 1989
Major Wins: 2 (The Open Championship 1969; U.S. Open 1970)

Langer

After turning professional in 1976, it took Bernhard Langer four years to win his first event (the 1980 Dunlop Masters). He then developed into one of the finest European golfers of a generation that included Faldo, Montgomerie and Ballesteros.

Although he is still playing, he is unlikely to add to his 91 professional wins, 42 of which came on the European Tour, placing him second overall behind Seve. For a golfer of his stature it is perhaps surprising that Langer only has two major championship wins to his name (both at the Masters, which he won in 1985 and 1993), although he famously battled the yips throughout his career. Indeed it was a missed six-foot putt on the 18th at Kiawah Island that gifted a half to Hale Irwin at the denouement of the 1991 Ryder Cup. The miss gave the Americans a one-point win rather than a tie that would have meant Europe retaining the trophy. The tournament itself was marred by poor sportsmanship and over exuberance from the U.S. team (a recurring theme), which

led to it being branded 'The War on the Shore'.

Although he weighed in with a couple of points at The Belfry two years later, the Americans were again too strong in the singles and they overturned a one-point deficit going into Sunday. He scored another brace in 1995 when the Europeans avenged the previous defeat and turned over a two-point deficit themselves, a rarity on a Sunday. At Valderrama two years later, Langer continued his good form and scored three vital points, the last of which was a nail-biting singles match against Brad

Right: *Bernhard Langer*

Faxon. When Colin Montgomerie secured a half at the last, Europe were home by the narrowest of margins.

The 2001 Ryder Cup was postponed until the following year due to the terrorist attacks in the United States, and Europe managed to wrest the trophy back after the unsavoury events at Brookline in 1999. Langer was inspirational with 3½ points as the Europeans recorded a comfortable three-point win. Langer's finest Ryder Cup moment came as the non-playing captain in 2004, however. Although the European side at home were always competitive, in the U.S. they had always struggled. At Oakland Hills, however, Langer's selection and tactics were carefully thought out and perfectly executed. His side was five points clear by Friday night, although Hal Sutton's team clawed a point back in the four-balls. The Clarke/Westwood, García/Donald and Harrington/McGinley partnerships then annihilated the American pairings and took them six points clear going into the singles. The Americans were then humiliated in the singles as Langer's side won by nine points, Europe's biggest winning margin since the tournament began in 1927. His overall record of six

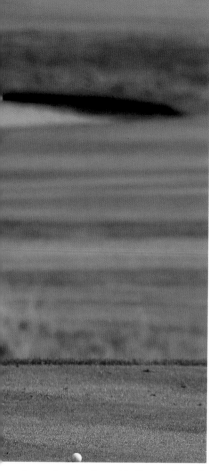

Bernhard Langer remains one of the most likeable players on the circuit. He was the first player to be officially ranked as number one under the new ranking system in 1986, he played for team Germany in the World Cup 13 times, and he also won the individual title in 1993.

Langer was inducted into the World Golf Hall of Fame in 2001, and in 2006 he was appointed as an honorary Officer of the Most Excellent Order of the British Empire in recognition of his contribution to the sport. In 2008 he took the European Senior Tour title and he has since amassed another 19 senior wins.

wins and a tie from 11 Ryder Cups is unsurpassed, and only Nick Faldo's 23 points keeps him ahead of Langer's 21.

Name: Bernhard Langer
Born: August 27th 1957, Anhausen, Germany
Ryder Cups: 1981, 1983, 1985, 1987, 1989, 1991, 1993, 1995, 1997, 2002, 2004 (as non-playing captain)
Ryder Cup Wins: 1985, 1987, tie 1989, 1995, 1997, 2002, 2004 (as non-playing captain)
Major Wins: 2 (U.S. Masters 1985, 1993)

Lyle

Although he was born in England, Sandy Lyle represented Scotland throughout his professional career. His father Alex introduced him to the game and the family home was just a short iron from Hawkstone Park Club in Shropshire. Sandy started playing aged three and he made his amateur debut at The Open aged 16 in 1974. He then won the amateur stroke-play championship in 1975 and 1977, and he turned professional after two appearances at the Walker Cup.

His first win came at the Nigeria Open in 1978, and he followed this up with his first European Tour title and a place on the 1979 Ryder Cup team. This was a period of transition for the Europeans, however, and the side simply wasn't as professional in ability, preparation or mentality as the Americans. After another humiliating defeat in 1981, Tony Jacklin was brought in to captain the side and revive their fortunes. Jacklin insisted that the team spare no expense on

preparation and, although they still came up agonisingly short in Florida, the shoots of recovery were visible at last.

At The Belfry in 1985 the hard work paid off and Lyle demolished Peter Jacobsen in the singles. Europe maintained the momentum and first Bernhard Langer and then Sam Torrance applied the coup de grace. Although he hadn't contributed much in the way of points in his previous outings, Lyle finally came good at Muirfield Village in 1987. He secured three points overall as the Europeans won on U.S. soil for the first time. This proved to be the watershed moment: European golf, so often the poorer cousin, was now able to compete on a level green on both sides of the pond.

Lyle's personal form was also improving: he took the 1985 Open, becoming the first British winner since Jacklin in 1969, and then played one of the great bunker shots on 18 during the final round of the 1988 Masters. The

shot secured him the coveted green jacket, thereby becoming the first Briton to win at Augusta.

Having not won a professional event for 19 seasons, Lyle rolled back the years in 2011 and took the ISPS Handa Senior World Championship in China, the 29th title of an illustrious career.

Name: Andrew Walter Barr 'Sandy' Lyle
Born: February 9th 1958, Shrewsbury, England
Ryder Cups: 1979, 1981, 1983, 1985, 1987
Ryder Cup Wins: 1985, 1987
Major Wins: 2 (Masters 1988; The Open Championship 1985)

Above: *Sandy Lyle escapes from a bunker*

McGinley

Few golfers are more identifiable with Europe's recent domination of the Ryder Cup than Paul McGinley. Despite modest individual success on the European Tour and in majors, McGinley seems to come alive when it comes to golf's greatest team event, and he will be Europe's captain at Gleneagles in September 2014.

McGinley had a promising future as a Gaelic footballer until a broken kneecap ended his career at 19. However, he turned this setback into a positive by focusing on his other sporting love. He played in the 1991 Walker Cup against an American side that included Phil Mickelson, before turning professional later that year.

McGinley took to the European Tour quite quickly, suffering two narrow playoff defeats in the 1993 French Open to Constantino Rocca and the 1994 Open Mediterrania against José María Olazábal. However, his first victory was finally secured at the 1996 Hohe Brucke Open.

Three more European Tour victories would follow, with his final victory to date coming in 2005's season-ending Volvo Masters at Spain's Valderrama Golf Club. McGinley started his final round four shots off the lead, but he then shot a superb 67 for the biggest individual tournament win of his career, finishing two strokes ahead of Ryder Cup team-mate Sergio Garcia. This victory also helped secure McGinley third place on the Order of Merit, his best finish to date.

However, there can be no doubt that it is with the Ryder Cup that McGinley will forever be identified. He cemented his place in European golfing folklore in his first appearance in the event at the Belfry in 2002 by holing the winning putt.

McGinley had trailed America's hitherto unbeaten Jim Furyk from the second hole and seemed an unlikely candidate for the starring role. Leading by one with two to play, Furyk looked to have the game in the bag. However, a birdie for the Irishman at 17 pulled things

level and the stage was set for a dramatic conclusion at the last.

McGinley was left with a tricky 10-foot putt to win both his match and the Ryder Cup, and he coolly rolled the putt home to kick-start the European celebration. Before the cup was handed over, a delirious McGinley draped himself in an Irish flag and threw himself into the lake at the 18th green.

He went on to represent Europe at Oakland Hills in 2004 and again at the K Club in 2006, making him the first European golfer to be a winner in every one of his three appearances. He was also an assistant to Colin Montgomerie at Celtic Manor in 2010 and José María Olazábal at Medinah in 2012, both of which resulted in dramatic European wins.

But the biggest task is still to come for the affable Dubliner, when, in September 2014, he succeeds José María Olazábal and becomes Ireland's first captain. McGinley's opposite number will be the legendary Tom Watson, back in charge at the age of 65.

Name: Paul McGinley
Born: December 16th 1966, Dublin, Ireland
Ryder Cups: 2002, 2004, 2006
Ryder Cup Wins: 2002, 2004, 2006
Major Wins: 0

McIlroy

Rory McIlroy's father, Gerry, was a noted amateur who began teaching his son to play when he was just 18 months old. He became the youngest member of his local club at just seven, and his first international victory came at the World Championships for Under-10s in Florida.

Aged 15, McIlroy was a member of the successful junior Ryder Cup team, and he backed up his early promise with amateur victories at the West of Ireland Championships and the European Championships in 2006. He also took the silver medal as leading amateur at the 2007 Open Championship despite fading from third place after his opening round.

He turned professional later the same year and finished 42nd in his first pro event, the British Masters. His first win came at the Dubai Desert Classic in 2009. He finished 20th in the 2009 Masters and 10th in the U.S. Open, but then made third at the U.S. PGA. There was now little doubt that a superstar was on the rise.

Since his first PGA Tour title, the 2010 Quail Hollow Championship, in which he became the first man since Tiger Woods to seal victory on the tour before his 21st birthday, he has notched up 11 more wins. He will also be remembered for equalling the course record with a nine-under-par 63 on the Old Course at St. Andrews in the opening round of the 2010 Open Championship, a tournament in which he eventually finished third. Later that year he won a crucial half point that helped secure the Ryder Cup for Europe.

His relationship with the Ryder Cup was uneasy at best, however. In 2009 he'd described it as an exhibition event and claimed taking part wasn't one of his goals. Having been part of the successful 2010 side, and with Colin Montgomerie's words – "the Ryder Cup will never be an exhibition, it's a unique and special event" – ringing in his ears, he wisely retracted his comments. He then secured three points to help Europe to the unlikeliest of victories at the 2012

Ryder Cup, which thereafter became known as the Miracle at Medinah. If he continues his good form, he looks certain to be part of the 2014 side in Gleneagles.

McIlroy might have won the 2011 Masters but for a final round of 80, the worst final day's play by anyone leading the tournament. He then silenced the doubters by winning the 2011 U.S. Open with a record aggregate score of 16 under par. In so doing he became the youngest player to win the title since Bobby Jones in 1923. In a year of superlatives, he then became the youngest player to earn $10 million on the PGA Tour and €10 million on the European Tour. More wins in 2012 saw him reach the coveted number one spot on the world rankings, and he then demolished the establishment to win the PGA by eight strokes.

He endured a torrid 2013 – probably due to troubles in his private life – although he did rally to win the Australian Open. He then won the prestigious 2014 BMW PGA Championship at Wentworth.

Above: *Rory McIlroy holds the trophy after winning the 111th US Open*

Name: Rory McIlroy
Born: May 4th 1989, Holywood, Northern Ireland
Ryder Cups: 2010, 2012
Ryder Cup Wins: 2010, 2012
Major Wins: 2 (U.S. Open 2011; PGA Championship 2012)

Montgomerie

Colin Montgomerie was raised in Yorkshire and schooled in golf by Bill Ferguson at the Ilkley Club. He won three amateur tournaments in his native Scotland: the 1983 Scottish Youths' Championship, the 1985 Scottish Stroke-play Championship, and the 1987 Scottish Amateur Championship. He also played for Scotland in the Eisenhower Trophy in 1984 and 1986, and for Great Britain & Ireland in the Walker Cup in 1985 and 1987.

Having turned professional in 1988, he was immediately named Rookie of the Year. His first win on the tour came at the Portuguese Open in 1989, which he took by eight shots. Two years later he made his debut in the Ryder Cup, a tournament with which he would eventually become synonymous, in much the same way as Seve before him.

It's difficult to overstate the impact Montgomerie had on European golf but he surely ranks alongside the greats of the sport. Between 1993 and 1999, he finished top of the Order of Merit and

spent almost eight years ranked among the world's top 10. He finished runner-up five times in major tournaments: the 1995 PGA Championship, the 1994, 1997 and 2006 U.S. Opens, and the 2005 Open Championship. He also won three consecutive Volvo PGA Championships at Wentworth, the unofficial fifth major.

Although he never won a major (and is probably the best player not to do so) his achievements at the Ryder Cup are staggering. Indeed, only Nick Faldo and Bernhard Langer can compare with his playing record and points' haul. He played in eight tournaments and never lost a singles match. He halved the last hole to win the cup for Europe at Valderrama in 1997, and sank the winning putt in Europe's demolition job at Oakland Hills in 2004. In overcoming extreme and unnecessary abuse from the American fans at Brookline in 1999, he showed great strength of character, albeit in a losing cause. (His opponent in the singles on Sunday, Payne Stewart, had stirred

Above: *Colin Montgomerie of Scotland*

the pot beforehand by saying that the European players were only fit to caddy for his side, but he was so embarrassed by the abuse Monty was receiving during the match that he limited the damage by graciously conceding on the 18th fairway.)

In captaining the 2010 side to victory at Celtic Manor, Montgomerie became the only person to have tasted victory as a player and captain in Europe's three main team golf events: the Ryder Cup, Seve Trophy and Royal Trophy.

Name: Colin Stuart Montgomerie
Born: June 23rd 1963, Glasgow, Scotland
Ryder Cups: 1991, 1993, 1995, 1997, 1999, 2002, 2004, 2006, 2010 (as non-playing captain)
Ryder Cup Wins: 1995, 1997, 2002, 2004, 2006, 2010 (as non-playing captain)
Major Wins: 0

O'Connor

Right: *Christy O'Connor Senior drives off the tee*

Christy O'Connor turned professional aged 22 but he didn't play at The Open Championship for another five years (1951). Despite finishing a creditable 19th on debut and then winning the 1956 and 1959 British Masters, he took the surprising decision not to play any major championships in the United States. The only real exposure he had to American courses, therefore, was as part of European Ryder Cup squad.

O'Connor set a record of 10 appearances at the event, which wasn't broken until Nick Faldo played in his 11th Ryder Cup in 1997. His first outing at the Thunderbird Country Club resulted in the hosts recording their seventh consecutive win. Two years later at Lindrick Golf Club in Rotherham, O'Connor and playing partner Eric Brown were hammered 7&5 in the foursomes but O'Connor then thrashed Dow Finsterwald 7&6 in the singles. Having taken 6½ points on the Saturday, the British team recorded its first win since 1933, although it would be the last until 1985 in what was a barren period for British golf.

O'Connor went on to win at least one professional event on the British Tour every year throughout the 1960s, and he was also Irish professional champion 10 times, the last of which came at the age of 53 in 1978. His best result at The Open was a second place in 1965. Had he not carded 73 and 74 in his middle rounds he would surely have pipped five-time champion Peter Thomson to the post.

He won the 1970 John Player Classic, then the richest prize in golf, before joining the soon-to-be lucrative Senior Tour.

Name: Christy O'Connor Senior
Born: December 21st 1924, Galway, Ireland
Ryder Cups: 1955, 1957, 1959, 1961, 1963, 1965, 1967, 1969, 1971, 1973
Ryder Cup Wins: 1957, tie 1969
Major Wins: 0

Olazábal

Nicknamed 'Ollie', José María Olazábal first made an impact as a junior in 1983 when he won three championships: the Italian Open Amateur Championship, the Spanish Open Amateur Championship, and the British Boys' Amateur Championship. The following year he took another three titles, the Amateur Championship, the Belgium International Youths' Championship, and the Spanish Open Amateur Championship. Following his 1985 British Youths' Amateur Championship win, Olazábal turned professional.

He managed 30 professional wins overall, including two majors, both at the Masters. He also spent more than five years in the top 10 of the world rankings, but it is perhaps for his performances at the Ryder Cup that he will be best remembered. He played for the European team seven times (of which he was on the winning side four times with a single tie) and was the captain who masterminded the incredible turnaround at Medinah in 2012.

His partnership was compatriot and lifelong friend Seve Ballesteros was the strongest European pairing of all time, the duo winning an incredible 12 points from 15 matches. Between them they dispatched American pairings of the quality of Strange/Kite, Nelson/Stewart and Watson/O'Meara with monotonous regularity, the latter by the incredible score of 6&5 at the Belfry in 1989. When the European fight-back finally condemned the Americans to defeat in 2012, Olazábal was completely overcome with emotion as he dedicated the victory to Seve.

In 2009 Olazábal was elected into the World Golf Hall of Fame. Four years later he became only the second golfer to be presented with Spain's prestigious Prince of Asturias Award.

Above: *Spain's José María Olazábal*

Name: José María Olazábal
Born: February 5th 1966, Hondarribia, Spain
Ryder Cups: 1987, 1989, 1991, 1993, 1997, 1999, 2006, 2012 (as non-playing captain)
Ryder Cup Wins: 1987, tie 1989, 1997, 2006, 2012 (as non-playing captain)
Major Wins: 2 (Masters 1994, 1999)

Oosterhuis

Undoubtedly one of Great Britain's greatest golfers, the 6'5" Peter Oosterhuis was a highly successful amateur, representing Great Britain against the United States in the 1967 Walker Cup and again in the 1968 World Amateur Team Championship.

He turned professional shortly afterwards and wasted no time in making his mark on the European scene and offering himself as a pretender to Tony Jacklin's crown as Britain's leading player. In 1970, he finished seventh in the Order of Merit, which included a tied sixth-place finish in the Open Championship at St. Andrews. The 22-year-old had rounds of 73, 69, 69 and 76 to finish the tournament at one under par, four strokes behind the winner Jack Nicklaus.

In the early years of his professional career he played on the European Tour, winning a formidable four consecutive Order of Merit titles from 1971 to 1974, a record that stood until 1997 when it was broken by Colin Montgomerie. In this time, he recorded wins in the 1973 British

PGA Championship, and consecutive victories at the 1973 and 1974 French Opens.

In 1973 he registered the greatest performance so far by a British player at The Masters, which he led after three rounds. A blistering final round of 68 from Tommy Aaron, however, saw him pipped at the post. Oosterhuis's joint third placing garnered the attention of the golfing world, and he wasn't finished there.

The following year he finished runner-up to Gary Player in The Open Championship. The following year he led the tournament at the halfway point, only to fade and finish an agonising three shots behind Tom Watson.

The same year, Oosterhuis decided to ply his trade on the US PGA Tour, where he competed until 1986. His most notable triumph came in the 1981 Canadian Open, where he held off the challenge of the great Jack Nicklaus to record a memorable win.

Oosterhuis had one last crack at the

title he wanted most – The Open – at Royal Troon in 1982. He gave Tom Watson a run for his money, but had to settle for a tie for second place with Nick Price, finishing just one stroke behind the American.

Despite playing in six losing teams, one could argue that Oosterhuis's Ryder Cup record is his most impressive achievement. He was unfortunate to compete in a period of American dominance but Oosterhuis still managed to compile an outstanding 15½ points.

He made his debut in 1971 at St. Louis and, after three straight defeats, Oosterhuis fought back splendidly to record three wins in his remaining three games. Included in those three victories was a memorable 3&2 success against Arnold Palmer in the afternoon singles. However, it was not enough to prevent the Americans recording an 18½-13½ victory.

He was back on Ryder Cup duty two years later, once again performing superbly. Oosterhuis gained four points from a possible six, although this was again not enough to stave off the usual defeat, 19-13.

Oosterhuis continued his fine Ryder Cup record in 1975, gaining 2½ points from five in a 21-11 defeat, but his finest Ryder Cup came in 1977, when he boasted a 100 per cent record thanks to

Above: *Peter Oosterhuis*

Right: *Peter Oosterhuis lines up a tricky putt*

two wins in partnership with England's new hope, Nick Faldo. In the singles, he eased to a two-up victory over Jerry McGee.

Oosterhuis played in two more Ryder Cups, losing once more in 1979, despite continuing his fruitful partnership with Faldo to record two wins out of three. His final appearance came in 1981, where a disappointing three defeats out of three dented his excellent record.

However, the impact he made at the Ryder Cup will stand the test of time. He is co-holder of the record for most wins in the singles with Faldo, Arnold Palmer, Billy Casper, Sam Snead and Lee Trevino (six). It was Oosterhuis's short game that caught the eye, his ability to get up and down from anywhere making him an opponent the Americans genuinely feared.

After he retired, Oosterhuis became a respected commentator. In 1994, he was hired by Sky Sports to cover the PGA Tour. The BBC then asked him to cover two Open Championships. From 1995 until 1997, he was the lead analyst for the Golf Channel's coverage of the European Tour, before becoming part of CBS Sports's team for the Masters and the PGA Championship. In 1998, he joined the CBS golf team fulltime.

Name: Peter Oosterhuis
Born: May 3rd, 1948; London, England
Ryder Cups: 1971, 1973, 1975, 1977, 1979, 1981
Ryder Cup Wins: 0
Major Wins: 0

Poulter

If there is one golfer who most embodies Europe's attitude to the Ryder Cup and its recent stranglehold on the competition, then it is Ian Poulter. It is Poulter's tenacity that sets him apart in the ultra-competitive world of professional golf, and particularly so in the Ryder Cup.

Poulter's astonishing self-belief has never wavered and despite still waiting to win his first major title, he is a player who boasts a bagful of titles, including two World Golf Championships. However, for so single-minded a sportsman, it is within the team environment that he prospers most, and boy has he prospered in the Ryder Cup.

Poulter made his debut at Oakland Hills in 2004, where, despite losing his four-balls with Darren Clarke, he effectively won his team the Ryder Cup with a birdie against Chris Riley on the 15th, guaranteeing him the half point that Europe needed for victory.

His arrival on the Ryder Cup scene was a seismic one, but poor form meant he missed out on the 2006 event at the K Club. His critics wondered if his love of the limelight was hindering his performances, but he roared back into the headlines in 2008 at Valhalla and was the one shining light in Nick Faldo's ill-fated reign as captain, the Europeans losing by their largest margin in years.

If 2008 proved to be Poulter's redemption in the public eye, his heroics in 2010 at Celtic Manor elevated him further. Graeme McDowell may have holed the winning putt, but there is no doubt that Europe would have lost if it wasn't for the talismanic Poulter.

Poulter had declared he would deliver a point, and was true to his word against Matt Kuchar, who had previously won two points out of three. The Americans had clawed their way back into the contest by winning the first two matches, but Poulter thrashed Kuchar 5&4, and with it gave Miguel Ángel Jiménez and Luke Donald the confidence to win their matches.

With three points out of four he was again Europe's leading scorer, and it was his Ryder Cup pedigree that ensured that he would be a wildcard pick two years later in Medinah, even if he didn't make the team on merit. And how Poulter justified captain José María Olazábal's faith.

With Europe trailing by a massive six points late on the Saturday afternoon, Poulter and Rory McIlroy rolled in five consecutive birdies to snatch a vital point from Jason Dufner and Zach Johnson. With Sergio García and Luke Donald also beating Tiger Woods and Steve Stricker, Europe were now only four points behind going into the final day, and Poulter's unwavering fervour fuelled the belief that Europe could pull off the unlikeliest of victories.

Poulter went one step further in assisting the greatest comeback, winning the last two holes to defeat U.S. Open champion Webb Simpson. As the rest of Europe's heroes kept on posting victories, it was left to Martin Kaymer to retain the cup for Europe, which he did in some style, finishing off a remarkable weekend for Europe and for Mr Ryder Cup himself.

As at Valhalla and Celtic Manor, Poulter was Europe's standout performer. But this time it felt like his achievement was even greater. No player has influenced the result of the Ryder Cup in the manner of Poulter in

2012. To many, the Miracle of Medinah was his victory more than anyone else's.

Poulter's four wins mean that his Ryder Cup record now reads won 12, lost three. He has played four singles and never lost. Incredibly, he has lost only once in his past 12 Ryder Cup encounters.

"I think the Ryder Cup should build a statue to him," said Olazábal before the match. After the dramatic ending, the chance of him being honoured by a sculptor became a near certainty.

Name: Ian James Poulter
Born: January 10th 1976, Hitchin, England
Ryder Cups: 2004, 2008, 2010, 2012
Ryder Cup Wins: 2004, 2010, 2012
Major Wins: 0

Rees

Right: *Dai Rees (1913-1983) on the eighth tee at Lindrick Golf Club*

Dai Rees has often been lauded as not only one of Britain's greatest ever golfers but also one of its most significant Ryder Cup figures. The winner of many prestigious tournaments both in Britain and abroad, Rees played in nine Ryder Cups.

However, it is as the captain of the Great Britain Ryder Cup team that defeated the United States at Yorkshire's Lindrick Golf Club in 1957 for which he is most famous. Significantly, the victory he helped orchestrate was Britain's only defeat of the United States in the competition between 1933 and 1985.

Rees played an integral part in the triumph alongside his playing partner Ken Bousfield. Their pairing deserves to be held in the same esteem as Ballesteros and Olazábal and Westwood and Clarke as, in the years prior to the 1960s, pairings with great track records were hard to come by.

Back then, there was only ever one series of foursomes per match (both the foursomes and singles were played over 36 holes). But in 1957 at Lindrick Rees and Bousfield stood in the way of a four-nil whitewash, with captain Rees resolutely believing that the match was still winnable.

They beat Art Wall and Fred Hawkins 3&2 and then both went on to win their

Overall, Rees recorded seven wins, no losses and one half, which was all the more impressive given that the British team suffered a succession of heavy defeats during his career. He was also considered to be one of the greatest British golfers never to win The Open Championship.

He finished runner-up three times, in 1953, 1954 and 1961, but perhaps his best chance of victory came in 1946, when he shot a final round 80 to slip into a tie for fourth place.

Rees died after a short illness in 1983, and his remains lie in the graveyard of St. Andrews Church close to the grave of the great Harry Vardon.

singles matches to help Great Britain to their seminal victory. In recognition of this achievement, Rees won the BBC Sports Personality of the Year award. The following year he was made a Commander of the Order of the British Empire.

Name: Dai Rees
Born: March 31st 1913, Glamorgan, Wales
Died: November 15th 1983, Barnet, London
Ryder Cups: 1937, 1947, 1949, 1951, 1953, 1955, 1957, 1959, 1961, 1967 (as non-playing captain)
Ryder Cup Wins: 1957
Major Wins: 0

Rocca

There is little doubt that Constantino Rocca is the greatest golfer Italy has ever produced. Now plying his trade on the European Senior Tour, the jovial Italian is a three-time Ryder Cup player and remains the only European to have beaten Tiger Woods in a singles match (he won 4&2 at Valderrama in 1997).

Yet, in many ways, it is remarkable that Rocca ever became a golfer. The son of a local quartz miner, he started caddying with his older brother at the age of seven, only to give it up after leaving school to work for a decade in a local plastics factory.

He was 24 before he finally made the decision to turn professional. He enjoyed little initial success and he had to make several trips to the qualifying school to retain his European Tour Card.

However, he finally made his mark on the game in the 1990s, and before long he was putting Italian golf on the map. By 1993, he had risen to sixth in the Order of Merit. Two years later he finished fourth and racked up five titles on the tour, the first of which was the 1993 Open de Lyon, and the most prestigious of which was the 1996 Volvo PGA Championship. It was at the 1995 Open Championship, however, that he would become a household name.

His sensational putt from 60 feet on the 18th green at St. Andrews to make the birdie he needed to force a playoff with eventual winner John Daly is one of the most memorable moments in major championship history. He famously celebrated by collapsing and pounding the turf with joy.

It was his impressive showing at The Open that helped Rocca qualify for the Ryder Cup the same year at Oak Hill. This was Rocca's second selection for the team and he was determined to put the memories of his first appearance behind him. (Fellow rookie Davis Love III beat him on the final hole to hand the cup to the Americans. The Italian had been one up with two to play but, after three-putting the 17th, his confidence deserted him and he could only bogey

Left: *Italy's greatest golfer and the only man to beat Tiger Woods in Ryder Cup singles, Constantino Rocca*

the final hole.)

In 1995, spurred on by the memories of defeat, Rocca played like a man possessed. By the final day's singles, he had already won three of his foursome and four-ball matches (two of which were against Love). Even though he then lost to Love in his singles match on the final day, Rocca still managed to grab the headlines by registering only the third hole-in-one in Ryder Cup history.

Rocca was on the winning side again in Valderrama two years later. Playing with José María Olazábal, Rocca contributed another three points, beginning with a four-ball and foursome win apiece against who else but Davis Love.

Then, desperate to put his two previous singles defeats behind him, Rocca finally exorcised his demons with a crucial 4&2 win over Tiger Woods. This was one of Woods's first losses in singles play and is still the only time a European has beaten him in a Ryder Cup singles match.

Rocca never played in another Ryder Cup, but his place in the event's history was already guaranteed. He boasts a 6-5-0 win-loss-half record, and a 53 per cent winning ratio in the cup is one of the best in European team history.

Name: Constantino Rocca
Born: December 4th 1956, Bergamo, Italy
Ryder Cups: 1993, 1995, 1997
Ryder Cup Wins: 1995, 1997
Major Wins: 0

Torrance

One of the most charismatic and competitive golfers to come out of Europe, it could be argued that no one has enjoyed their Ryder Cup experience more than Samuel Robert Torrance. When the tournament was staring into the abyss as a result of America's dominance, Torrance was one of the men responsible for resurrecting the Ryder Cup.

Coached by his father Bob from childhood, Torrance turned professional at 16 and joined the European Tour the following year. It wasn't long before he achieved his first professional win in 1972, before going on to win the Sir Henry Cotton Rookie of the Year award in the same year. He had to wait a little longer for his first European Tour win, which he secured by lifting the Piccadilly Medal in 1976.

Renowned for his long driving, accurate short iron play and buccaneering style, Torrance's best finish on the European Tour Order of Merit was second, which he achieved twice, first in 1984 and again in 1995. In total he won 21 times on the European Tour having played at more than 700 events.

Yet it was the Ryder Cup that brought the best out of the passionate Scot. More naturally suited to the team dynamic than the classic introspective golfer racking up the majors, Torrance's first appearance came in 1981 at Surrey's Walton Heath Golf Club. He wasn't the only novice, as Germany's Bernhard Langer and Spaniards José María Cañizares and Manuel Piñero were also making their Ryder Cup debuts.

The Americans were, once more, in a different class, running out emphatic winners, but it was in the next fixture two years later that the tide finally began to turn. A one-point loss in Florida, with Europe captained by Tony Jacklin and revitalised by the return of Seve Ballesteros, served notice to the golfing world that Europe would no longer roll over.

So it proved when, in 1985 at The Belfry, the stage was set for the Europe's first victory in 28 years. And who else but Torrance would be responsible for the wining putt.

The Scot was facing U.S. Open champion Andy North and had fallen three holes behind. But Torrance fought back to all-square going to the 18th and, after North's ball found water, Torrance made birdie by holing an 18-foot putt. The emotional Scot, who had been in tears beforehand, raised his arms to signal the Ryder Cup was back in European hands.

Torrance wasn't finished there. He made history as a member of the first European team to win on U.S. soil at Muirfield Village in 1987 and he went on play in four more Ryder Cups. Then, in 2002, Torrance was chosen to captain Europe, the first time the sides had met since the controversial tournament at Brookline in 1999. The row had rumbled on, with many questioning whether the spirit of Ryder Cup matches would ever be the same. Europe's underdogs produced one of the most outstanding singles displays in recent Ryder Cups to beat the United States comprehensively.

With the scores tied at 8-8 after the four-balls and foursomes, Torrance took a big risk by sending his best players out first on the final day. But the gamble paid off handsomely and Europe wrestled back the trophy. Victory made him the second European captain to sink the winning putt and captain a winning team at separate Ryder Cups, after Seve Ballesteros in 1987 (as a player) and 1997 (as captain), and cemented his Ryder Cup legacy for eternity. Torrance modestly played down his role in the triumph: "I just led them to the water, and they drank copiously."

Above: *Sam Torrance, the man whose putt secured Europe's first Ryder Cup in 28 years in 1985*

> **Name:** Samuel Robert Torrance
> **Born:** August 24th 1953, Largs, Scotland
> **Ryder Cups:** 1981, 1983, 1985, 1987, 1989, 1991, 1993, 1995, 2002 (as non-playing captain)
> **Ryder Cup Wins:** 1985, 1987, tie 1989, 1995, 2002 (as non-playing captain)
> **Major Wins:** 0

Westwood

Right: *Lee Westwood during practice*

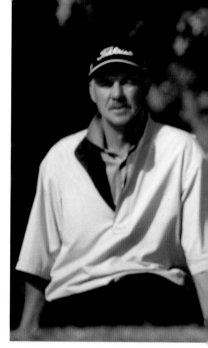

Lee Westwood started playing golf at 13 and he soon won the Junior Championship of Nottinghamshire. He took his first amateur tournament in 1990, won the Peter McEvoy Trophy, and then won the 1993 British Youth Championship before turning professional. Three years later, Westwood won his first pro tournament, the 1996 Volvo Scandinavian Masters, and he followed this up with victory in the Sumitomo VISA Taiheiyo Masters in Japan.

From 1998 until 2001 he spent more than 180 weeks in the top 10 of the Official World Golf Rankings, and was listed again at the end of 2008 and into 2009. Westwood has also been named European Tour Golfer of the Year three times, in 1998, 2000 and 2009. During that time he has accumulated 40 wins, although he is one of the best golfers never to win a major.

His best results in the major championships include third place at the 2008 and 2011 U.S. Opens, joint third at the 2009 PGA Championship, and, in 2010, he came second at The Masters and The Open Championship. Later in the year he ended Tiger Woods's stint at the top of the world rankings when he became the first British golfer to be ranked number one since Nick Faldo in 1994.

It is as a team player that Westwood has made his biggest contribution to the sport. He has played in eight Ryder Cups, of which six have been European victories. He only scored two points at

including dismantling the ill-thought-out pairing of Woods and Mickelson. Four more points at the K Club in 2006 condemned the U.S. team to another humiliating defeat, but they were able to exploit Faldo's tactical naivety in 2008 and exact revenge.

Westwood secured another 2½ points at Celtic Manor in 2010 as a Montgomerie-inspired Europe regained the trophy by the narrowest of margins. He then delivered a crucial two points as Europe staged the greatest fight-back in golfing history at Medinah in 2012. Trailing by four points going into what was traditionally their weakest day, Europe took 8½ points from 12 to complete the miracle recovery.

Valderrama in 1997 but a strong European side inspired by Seve Ballesteros and José María Olazábal saw off the American challenge. He scored another brace in Brookline two years later but the Americans turned a four-point deficit going into the singles into a one-point win. His excellent pairing with Sergio García at The Belfry in 2002 yielded three points as Europe romped home, and he delivered an incredible 4½-point return in the comfortable win at Oakland Hills,

Name:	Lee John Westwood
Born:	April 24th 1973, Worksop, England
Ryder Cups:	1997, 1999, 2002, 2004, 2006, 2008, 2010, 2012
Ryder Cup Wins:	1997, 2002, 2004, 2006, 2010, 2012
Major Wins:	0

Whitcombe

Right: *(l-r) Golfing siblings Reg, Ernest and Charles Whitcombe were all members of the 1935 Ryder Cup team*

Charles Whitcombe was the middle brother of successful golfing siblings (younger brother Reg won the 1938 Open Championship at Sandwich). He was a late developer but still finished fifth in the 1922 Open, although he repeatedly failed to beat the very best – Hagen, Jones, Sarazen and Cotton – to claim one of the majors. The closest he came was in 1935 when finished on level par and tied for third behind Alf Perry and Alf Padgham at Muirfield. Two years later he came fourth in Carnoustie after shooting a final round of 76 when a 71 (par) would have given him victory.

He was more successful in the Ryder Cup, captaining the side four times and tasting victory with Britain at Moortown in Leeds in 1929 and Southport in 1933. In the latter, he and Archie Compston halved their foursomes, and then Whitcombe annihilated Johnny Farrell 8&6 in the crucial singles on the Saturday. He only secured a half with Percy Alliss in the foursomes in Southport but it was enough for the British to win by a point.

Buoyed by these successes, Whitcombe won the PGA Matchplay title in 1928 and 1930, as well as the 1930 Irish Open.

Name: Charles Albert Whitcombe
Born: September 21st 1895, Somerset, England
Died: 1981
Ryder Cups: 1927, 1929, 1931 (as captain), 1933, 1935 (as captain), 1937 (as captain), 1949 (as non-playing captain)
Ryder Cup Wins: 1929, 1933
Major Wins: 0

Woosnam

Ian Woosnam took up golf at the Llanymynech Golf Club in Wales. He then played in regional competitions in Shropshire alongside fellow amateur Sandy Lyle. He turned professional in 1976, joined the European Tour three years later and won his first professional title at the 1982 Swiss Open, a year in which he also placed eighth in the Order of Merit. Woosnam would go on to finish in the top 10 a total of 13 times between 1983 and 1997.

For a player of sublime skill who could long-drive with the best, it was perhaps a surprise that he only had one major championship success: The Masters in 1991. In what was a golden era for British golf, Faldo and Lyle helped ensure that the green jacket spent four years in the UK. Woosnam reached number one in the world rankings after his victory at Augusta and remained at the top for a year. He might well have won a second major at the 2001 Open but his caddie forgot to remove a club and he was penalised two shots for having 15 clubs in his bag (he eventually finished third).

Woosnam made the Ryder Cup squad eight times and was selected as non-playing captain in 2006. He was an integral member of a team that dominated the event, and he helped Europe to four outright victories and a tie as a player, as well as leading the team to victory at the K Club in 2006. Although he never won a singles match, his record of 14 wins and five halves from 31 matches compares favourably with all but a few of his peers.

He has also represented Wales at the World Cup 14 times (he won the competition individually and as part of the team in 1987). In 2007 Woosnam was awarded an OBE in the New Year's Honours List. He ended his career with 50 professional wins, 29 of which were on the European Tour.

Above: *Ryder Cup Captain Ian Woosnam kisses the Ryder Cup trophy*

> **Name:** Ian Harold Woosnam
> **Born:** March 2nd 1958, Oswestry, Wales
> **Ryder Cups:** 1983, 1985, 1987, 1989, 1991, 1993, 1995, 1997, 2006 (as non-playing captain)
> **Ryder Cup Wins:** 1985, 1987, tie 1989, 1995, 1997, 2006 (as non-playing captain)
> **Major Wins:** 1 (Masters 1991)

Casper

Considered by many to be the most underrated golfer in the sport's history, and universally regarded as the game's greatest putter, Billy Casper played in the era of the so-called Big Three – Jack Nicklaus, Arnold Palmer, and Gary Player – who are widely credited with globally popularising the game. However, between 1964 and 1970 Casper won 27 tournaments on the PGA Tour – two more than Nicklaus and six more than Palmer and Player combined.

Casper was seen as the quiet man of the game, his ultra-efficient playing style and low-key nature contrasting with the sport's more charismatic giants. Yet there was nobody in golf who dared underestimate him.

The winner of two U.S. Opens and one Masters, the prolific Casper won 51 PGA Tour events in all during his illustrious career and boasts the third-longest winning streak on the tour: 16 straight seasons from 1956 to 1971. Only Arnold Palmer and Jack Nicklaus, both

on 17, won more.

The first of Casper's majors came in 1959, when he won the U.S. Open by one stroke at Winged Foot Golf Club in New York. However, it was his second U.S. Open triumph seven years later that would prove to be the most memorable, when Casper staged one of the greatest comebacks in golfing history, erasing a seven-stroke deficit on the final nine holes to tie with Arnold Palmer. Casper was then victorious in the 18-hole playoff to secure his second major.

His final major came at Augusta in 1970, where Casper again prevailed in an 18-hole play-off, this time against Gene Littler.

However, if Casper's individual record is impressive, his Ryder Cup record is unprecedented. Put simply, Casper boasts the best Ryder Cup record of any American golfer in the history of the event. He was a member of eight unbeaten Ryder Cup teams (seven wins and one tie) and has won more points than any other American player in history

(23½). Only one man (Palmer) has won more matches than Casper, and no one has won more singles matches.

In 1979, Casper was the non-playing captain of the United States team, in which a new dawn for the Ryder Cup had arrived with players from Europe, and not just Great Britain & Ireland, challenging America for the first time.

Despite having the likes of Spanish tyro Seve Ballesteros on the team, Casper's team were simply too strong for Europe. His side grabbed a handy three-point lead on the first day and, inspired by Larry Nelson, they never looked back,

retaining the cup comfortably 17-11.

This was the last Ryder Cup Casper would be involved in, cementing a simply staggering record in the event.

Name: William Earl Casper
Born: June 24th 1931, California, USA
Ryder Cups: 1961, 1963, 1965, 1967, 1969, 1971, 1973, 1975, 1979 (as non-playing captain)
Ryder Cup Wins: 1961, 1963, 1967, tie 1969, 1971, 1973, 1975, 1979 (as non-playing captain)
Major Wins: 3 (U.S. Open 1959, 1966; Masters 1970)

Couples

Fred Couples played golf throughout his childhood and, by the time he was at university, he was representing the Houston Cougars. He turned pro in 1980 and won his first PGA Tour event at the Kemper Open in 1983. He's since won another 14 PGA Tour events from a total of 57 professional wins, which includes 10 on the Seniors Tour. He won The Players Championship twice (in 1984 and 1996) and in 1992 he also became the first American to reach number one in the Official World Golf Rankings. He remained at the top spot for 16 weeks.

In 1991 and 1992, Couples was named PGA Tour Player of the Year, by which time he'd finally managed to shake a choker's tag that had dogged his early career. Indeed his mistake at the 1989 Ryder Cup – he hit an awful 9-iron approach to the 18th when a half would have secured the trophy – only enforced this opinion. (European team captain Tony Jacklin reportedly instructed Christy O'Connor simply to

hit the green and Couples would blow it, which is exactly what happened.) His win at the 1992 Masters went some way to exorcising the ghost, however, as did a point at the 1993 Ryder Cup at The

could only manage a final-round 71 to finish tied for third behind Phil Mickelson and Tim Clark.

In 2010, Couples made his debut on the Champions Tour in Hawaii. He again narrowly missed out on victory and eventually came second to Tom Watson. He did, however, win the following three stages and became the first golfer in the history of the Champions Tour to win three out of four events in his first year. He also came sixth at the 2010 Masters, his 26th top-10 finish in the major tournaments.

Couples is renowned for being one of the most laid-back players. He also earned the nickname 'Boom Boom' because of his monstrous drives.

Belfry.

Couples endured a lean period in the late-1990s but then returned to form at the 2006 Masters. Now 46, he remained in contention until the last few holes but

Name:	Frederick Steven Couples
Born:	October 3rd 1959, Seattle, Washington, USA
Ryder Cups:	1989, 1991, 1993, 1995, 1997
Ryder Cup Wins:	tie 1989, 1991, 1993
Major Wins:	1 (U.S. Masters 1992)

Dickinson

Opposite: *The incomparable Gardner Dickinson*

In Ben Hogan, Gardner Dickinson had the finest role model and mentor so he crafted his swing on the former champion's. He played for Louisiana State while still at college, and he and Jay Herbert delivered the 1947 national championship. He consigned the great Sam Snead to second place when taking his first PGA Tour title, the 1956 West Palm Beach Open, and it seemed that the early promise would lead to great things in the grand slams.

Dickinson didn't enjoy much success in the majors however – his best finish at the Masters was a lowly 10th in 1973, while he also only managed sixth at the 1967 U.S. Open and fifth at the 1965 PGA – and he only secured five top-10 finishes in a 22-year professional career. But as a member of the victorious 1967 and 1971 Ryder Cup teams he was virtually untouchable.

In the 1967 event at the Champions Club in Houston, he and Arnold Palmer beat Peter Alliss and Christy O'Connor Senior in the Friday morning foursomes and then demolished Malcolm Gregson and Hugh Boyle (5&4) in the afternoon. Paired with Doug Sanders for the Saturday four-balls, Dickinson delivered another two points, and he then beat Tony Jacklin in the singles. Such was the American dominance that they won by the embarrassing margin of 15 points.

At the Old Warson Country Club in 1971, Dickinson delivered near-faultless golf alongside playing partner Arnold Palmer (three points from three). He then thrashed O'Connor 5&4 in the Sunday morning singles only to lose his perfect Ryder Cup record by narrowly losing to Harry Bannerman in the afternoon. He then went on to found the Senior (now Champions) PGA Tour.

Name: Gardner Edward Dickinson
Born: September 14th 1927, Alabama, USA
Died: April 19th 1998, Florida, USA
Ryder Cups: 1967, 1971
Ryder Cup Wins: 1967, 1971
Major Wins: 0

Floyd

A giant of American golf, Ray Floyd's longevity in the game was matched only by his success, and even now, at 72, he will be part of the Ryder Cup action, serving as an assistant to Tom Watson at Gleneagles.

After leaving college, Floyd turned professional in 1961, and he quickly established himself on the PGA Tour. His first victory came two years later aged just 20 at the St. Petersburg Open Invitational. This was the first of his incredible 22 wins on the PGA Tour, which included four majors.

Famed for his outstanding short game, Floyd won the first of his majors at the 1969 PGA Championship at NCR Country Club in Dayton, Ohio, defeating the great Gary Player for a one-shot victory.

Seven years later at Augusta, Floyd put on a magnificent performance, winning The Masters by eight strokes. His 271 aggregate score tied the tournament record set by Jack Nicklaus in 1965. Floyd captured a second PGA in 1982 at

Southern Hills in Tulsa, winning by three shots over another Ryder Cup great, Lanny Wadkins.

Finally, in 1986, Floyd registered perhaps his most emotional victory, capturing the U.S. Open at Shinnecock Hills Country Club. After three rounds, he was tied for fifth place, three shots behind leader Greg Norman. The Australian faltered on the Sunday, but Floyd shot 66 to register a dramatic two-stroke win over Wadkins again, and Chip Beck. Aged 44, he was, until Hale Irwin's dramatic 1990 triumph, the oldest winner of the tournament.

The one major title that eluded Floyd, which prevented him from completing the career grand slam, was The Open Championship. His best result came at St. Andrews in 1978, where he tied for second place behind Jack Nicklaus.

Floyd came close to winning two further Masters, first after losing a play-off to Nick Faldo in 1990, and then finishing runner-up again in 1992 behind Fred Couples. Floyd's final win on the PGA

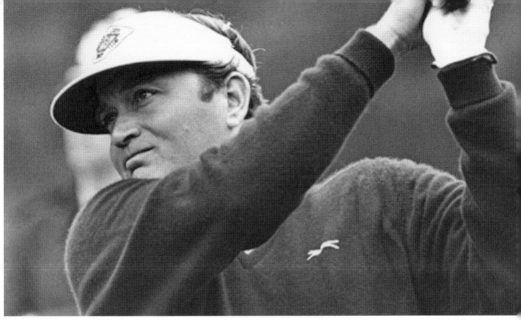

Tour came at the Doral-Ryder Open in 1992 at the age of 49, making him one of the oldest players to win a PGA Tour event.

Floyd served on a record eight U.S. Ryder Cup teams, an accolade he shares with Lanny Wadkins, Billy Casper and Phil Mickelson, while only 10 American players have scored more points in Ryder Cup matches.

He captained the United States team in 1989, tying the match with Jacklin's Europeans at The Belfry. In 1993, at Kiawah Island, Floyd became the oldest

player to compete in the Ryder Cup aged 51, inspiring his younger cohorts to a famous win.

Above: *Ray Floyd in 1977*

Name: Raymond Loran Floyd
Born: September 4th 1942, North Carolina, USA
Ryder Cups: 1969, 1975, 1977, 1981, 1983, 1985, 1989 (as non-playing captain), 1991, 1993
Ryder Cup Wins: tie 1969, 1975, 1977, 1981, 1983, tie 1989, 1991, 1993
Major Wins: 4 (U.S. Open 1986; Masters 1976; U.S. PGA 1969, 1982)

Furyk

Jim Furyk was renowned for his consistency at the major championships – he achieved top-10 finishes in at least one major in all but a handful of seasons since 1996. In 2006, he reached number two in the Official Golf World Rankings. Between 1999 and 2009 he also spent more than 300 weeks in the top ten.

Following in his father's footsteps (he was the club pro at Uniontown Country Club near Pittsburgh), Furyk started playing golf as a youngster. He then won the golfing state championship at high school before graduating from Arizona University and then turning professional in 1992. He had an unconventional looping swing so his supporters nicknamed him The Grinder.

Having won his first PGA Tour event in 1995 at the Las Vegas Invitational, Furyk went on to win at least one tournament every year from 1998 to 2003. He was also an integral part of the winning Ryder Cup sides of 1999 and 2008. In the former tournament, which became known as the Battle of Brookline after the unsavoury finish, the Americans were four points behind going into Sunday's singles. They then won the first six matches to take a narrow lead. Jim Furyk then upset the in-form Sergio García to give the Americans their eighth point of the day. When Justin Leonard halved his match with José María Olazábal, the U.S. team had completed one of the greatest sporting turnarounds in history. Although Olazábal could have holed his putt on the 17th green and kept European hopes alive, Leonard sank a monster and the team invaded the course while the Spaniard was lining up his putt. In 2008 Furyk secured 2½ points as an unfancied American side outthought and out manoeuvred a strong European team to romp home by five points.

He now has 26 professional tour wins, including his only major championship, the 2003 U.S. Open. He won the PGA Transitions Championship and the Verizon Heritage Tournament in 2010, and also took the Tour Championship. He has since come close to adding to his titles but, although he was leading the 2012 U.S. Open deep into the last day, he then

inexplicably hooked into the trees on 16. He was a shot clear during the final round of the 2013 PGA before being overhauled by Jason Dufner. In September 2013 he became only the sixth player to shoot a 59 in a PGA Tour event.

Name: James Michael Furyk
Born: May 12th 1970, Pennsylvania, USA
Ryder Cups: 1997, 1999, 2002, 2004, 2006, 2008, 2010, 2012
Ryder Cup Wins: 1999, 2008
Major Wins: 1 (U.S. Open 2003)

Hagen

Nicknamed 'Sir Walter' and 'The Haig', Hagen was a golfing pioneer during the first half of the 20th century. His 11 major championships place him third behind Tiger Woods (14) and Jack Nicklaus (18). He was the first American to win The Open Championship (1922) and the first man to captain his side at the Ryder Cup (1927).

Before turning professional in 1912, Hagen spent his early years caddying and playing at the Country Club of Rochester in his home state. He was the standout player by his late teens and he continued to represent the club having turned professional.

The boundary between amateur and professional golf during Hagen's era was not as defined as it is today. Professionals were often treated poorly at clubhouses, and many were banned from using the facilities or even refused entry. With his good looks, outrageous wardrobe and charisma, Hagen raised the status of professional golf and dragged it into a modern era in which players could appear in lucrative exhibitions as well as the paying events, and endorse products to further raise their profiles. It is often said that he became sport's first millionaire on the back of sound investments.

As a team player, Hagen was the Ryder Cup captain for the first six events, of which he played in five. Hagen secured two points for his country in the inaugural match, and a strong side that included Gene Sarazen made short work of the Great Britain team. In 1929 Hagen won his foursome match alongside Johnny Golden but he was then annihilated 10&8 by opposing team captain George Duncan in atrocious conditions in Leeds. Hagen avenged the heavy defeat two years later in Columbus, Ohio, as the U.S. ran out comfortable 9-3 victors.

In 1933 Hagen took a strong side to Southport but the British team squeezed home by a point. It would be their last victory for 24 years. The Ridgewood Country Club in New Jersey was the venue for the 1935 Ryder Cup and Hagen again chipped in with a point

to help the U.S. to an easy 9-3 win. Although he was captain again in 1937 for the trip back to Southport, Hagen elected not to play. A side that included Sarazen, Byron Nelson and Sam Snead cruised to victory, the first time the hosts had been defeated since the tournament's inception.

Hagen enjoyed 75 professional wins, 45 of which were on the PGA Tour. He died in Michigan in 1969 at the age of 76 and was inducted into the World Golf Hall of Fame in 1974. Consistently voted into the top 10 golfers of all-time, he remains one of the game's greatest players, an innovator, visionary, stylist and entrepreneur.

Above: *Walter Hagen*

> **Name:** Walter Charles Hagen
> **Born:** December 21st 1892, New York, USA
> **Died:** October 6th 1969, Michigan, USA
> **Ryder Cups:** 1927, 1929, 1931, 1933, 1935, 1937 (as non-playing captain)
> **Ryder Cup Wins:** 1927, 1931, 1935, 1937 (as non-playing captain)
> **Major Wins:** 11 (U.S. Open 1914, 1919; The Open Championship 1922, 1924, 1928, 1929; U.S. PGA 1921, 1924, 1925, 1926, 1927)

Hogan

Nicknamed 'The Hawk' and 'Bantam Ben', Ben Hogan played professional golf from 1930 until 1971. With nine majors and 59 more wins, he is rightly considered to be one of the greatest players in the history of the game. Hogan also made key observations about how to perfect a golf swing and wrote many books on technique and tactics. For these reasons, he is often credited with being the greatest ball striker of all.

Hogan had a difficult childhood and his father committed suicide when he was just nine. He dropped out of high school in 1930 but devoted his time and talents to golf and became a professional six months before his 18th birthday. His first ten years on the tour were difficult and he declared himself bankrupt more than once. He didn't win his first pro tournament until 1940, a year in which he won three consecutive events in North Carolina.

A late-blossoming career was interrupted by World War II but things didn't get much easier after the conflict.

He spent two months in hospital when his car struck a Greyhound bus head on in fog in 1949. He then made an incredible comeback despite being told that a double fracture of the pelvis as well as many more fractures and near-fatal blood clots might leave him unable to walk let alone play golf.

In 1953 Hogan was back to his dazzling best and it became his annus mirabilis. He couldn't enter all four majors as the Open and PGA overlapped but he was triumphant in Carnoustie, which, when added to the U.S. Open and Masters gave him an unprecedented clean sweep of the available majors, a so-called 'Hogan Slam'. It was perhaps the finest single season in golf until Tiger Woods won three majors in 2000. Hogan also founded his golf club company later that year. It was sold to American Machine & Foundry in 1960 but Hogan remained chairman of the board. Although the company was sold several times over the following decades, the Ben Hogan line was only discontinued in 2008.

Hogan's exploits at the Ryder Cup were equally impressive. He led the team in 1947 in the first event after the war and guided them to an emphatic 11-1 win. Two years later he chose not to play as he was still recovering from the accident (had he not leaned across to shield his wife, he would have been killed as the steering column punched through the driver's seat). He still masterminded a U.S. fight-back in the singles to win the cup 7-5.

He scored two points for his team at Pinehurst in 1951 as the United States routed the British once again. Despite his achievements in 1953, Hogan chose not to compete at Wentworth, and he then effectively retired from Ryder Cup play until returning as a non-playing captain in 1967. Although the scoring system has changed over the years, his side's 15-point winning margin remains the largest in the tournament's history.

Overall, it's difficult to compare players from different eras but Hogan – the only golfer to win the Masters, U.S. Open and Open Championship in the same year, only the second golfer to win all four majors, and a man who, at the age of 54 shot a record 30 on the back nine at Augusta (a mark that stood for 25 years) – would surely have been able to compete with Hagen, Nicklaus and Woods.

Above: *Ben Hogan*

Name: William Ben Hogan
Born: August 13th 1912, Stephenville, USA
Died: July 25th 1997, Fort Worth, Texas, USA
Ryder Cups: 1947, 1949 (as non-playing captain), 1951, 1967 (as non-playing captain)
Ryder Cup Wins: 1947, 1949 (as non-playing captain), 1951, 1967 (as non-playing captain)
Major Wins: 9 (U.S. PGA 1946, 1948; U.S. Open 1948, 1950, 1951, 1953; U.S. Masters 1951, 1953; The Open Championship 1953)

Irwin

Renowned for his wonderful iron play and single-minded pursuit of victory, Hale Irwin is undoubtedly one of America's greatest players. With a reputation as an outstanding golfer on both tough courses and under tough conditions, Irwin's legacy is secure. However, with five wins out of five in Ryder Cup matches, Irwin's impact on the U.S. Ryder Cup team also tells its own story.

Irwin lies 10th on his side's all-time points won category, while only five players have won more foursome matches, and eight players more four-ball matches.

The Missouri-born Irwin started playing aged four and he was only 14 when he first broke 70. He attended the University of Colorado, where he won the 1967 NCAA Championship. But Irwin was also a terrific American Football player, and was a two-time All-Big Eight defensive back.

However, it was golf that Irwin set his sporting sights on, and he turned professional in 1968, notching his first PGA Tour win just three years later. And this was just the start. Between 1974 and 1977, Irwin had four consecutive top-five finishes at The Masters, but it was his maiden major win, secured in 1974, that put him on the golfing map.

The 1974 U.S. Open came to be known as 'The Massacre at Winged Foot' for the incredibly tough conditions and correspondingly high scores. Irwin was the sole survivor, his winning score of seven over par secured after hitting a famous two-iron approach to the final green.

Irwin won a second U.S. Open in 1979 at Ohio's Inverness Club, finishing two strokes ahead of former champions Jerry Pate and Gary Player, but he had to wait 11 years for his third, and most famous, U.S. Open title, where he also produced one of the game's defining moments.

At the 1990 U.S. Open it was the 45-year-old Irwin's victory lap around the 18th green – a seemingly out-of-character display of emotion that included high-fiving spectators – which fans most remember. The celebration followed a 45-

Above: *Three-time U.S. Open winner Hale Irwin*

foot birdie putt that got him into an 18-hole playoff against Mike Donald, a playoff that Irwin needed one further hole (19 holes in total) to win.

In addition to his three U.S. Open wins, Irwin twice won the World Match Play Championship. His final PGA Tour win came in 1994 at the age of 48. Two years later, he joined the Champions Tour, where he became the dominant player in the tour's history, setting numerous records for scoring, money and victories.

Irwin's first four Ryder Cup matches all ended in emphatic victory. However, he would have to wait another 10 years before he would make his fifth and final appearance. In the meantime, the tide had turned in Europe's favour and, under Dave Stockton's jingoistic captaincy, the United States were desperate for a win at Kiawah Island.

After three days of 'Desert Storm'-fuelled acrimony, it was all down to the final singles match between Irwin and Bernhard Langer. Langer needed to win the 18th to secure a half, which would have meant Europe retaining the cup because of a draw.

What transpired was the tensest finish in the match's history. Irwin received a huge break off the tee, with his snap hook bouncing off a spectator. However, all Langer needed was a six-footer for victory, but it slipped by and Irwin secured the win his side needed, a fitting way to cap a glorious career.

Name: Hale Irwin
Born: June 3rd 1945, Missouri, USA
Ryder Cups: 1975, 1977, 1979, 1981, 1991
Ryder Cup Wins: 1975, 1977, 1979, 1981, 1991
Major Wins: 3 (U.S. Open 1974, 1979, 1990)

Kite

One of the most consistent golfers to have played the game, Texan legend Tom Kite's professional career spanned three decades and saw him play in seven Ryder Cups.

The Ryder Cup was so engrossing in the late 1980s and early 1990s, not only because of Seve, Jacklin, Faldo and co, but also because the Americans suddenly took the match seriously, and nobody embodied this attitude more than Kite. He never lost in seven singles matches and accumulated 17 points from his seven appearances.

Famous for his large glasses and precise swing, Kite was a university friend of fellow Ryder Cup stalwart Ben Crenshaw, who he also tied with to share the 1972 NCAA Championship. He turned professional later that year before bagging his first PGA victory in 1976. Another win followed in 1978 before his career took off with the dawn of the new decade.

Few players matched Kite's consistency, with most of his 19 career victories coming in the 1980s. He won the Vardon Trophy for low-scoring average in 1981 and 1982; was the PGA Tour's leading money winner in 1981 and 1989; and its Player of the Year in 1989. However, for many years, critics believed that Kite would end up as the best player to have never won a major.

He had tied for second place at the 1978 Open Championship, and repeated the feat alongside his lifelong friend Crenshaw at the 1983 Masters, losing by four strokes to Seve Ballesteros. His third runner-up spot came in the 1986 Masters, scene of Jack Nicklaus's glorious final major. However, he finally broke his duck at Pebble Beach in the 1992 U.S. Open.

Kite's two-stroke win over compatriot Jeff Sluman was hugely popular, and with the pressure finally off, his final years on the tour saw him snag two more PGA wins and another runner-up spot in the 1997 Masters, albeit 12 shots behind Tiger Woods.

Kite's prodigious record in the Ryder Cup more than matches his individual

Left: *Mr Consistent himself - Tom Kite*

successes. In his seven Ryder Cups, only seven American players have played more matches, only seven have accumulated more points and only four have recorded more fourball points.

Yet, it is in singles matches where Kite has the most impressive return: six points out of seven. He was on the winning team in his first three matches, and didn't taste defeat until Europe's seminal 1985 triumph.

Despite coming up short at Muirfield Village in 1987, Kite wasn't on a losing team again. After tying in 1989 and then missing the Kiawah Island 'War on the Shore', he was back to enjoy one last moment of glory in 1993's Belfry victory.

Kite was also involved in one of the event's greatest individual matches, when he took on Sandy Lyle in 1981. Kite won the match 3&2, but that doesn't tell the full story. In 16 holes Lyle had eight birdies and Kite 10. "If Sandy and I had played as a foursome, we would have beaten the lights out of anyone," Kite said.

Kite was honoured to be named America's captain for the 1997 match at Valderrama, while his opposing number was European talisman Seve Ballesteros. Kite's team ran the Europeans incredibly close on the final day, but a superb opening two days gave the home side the platform they needed to claim a narrow victory.

Name: Thomas Oliver Kite
Born: December 9th 1949, Texas, USA
Ryder Cups: 1979, 1981, 1983, 1985, 1987, 1989, 1993, 1997 (as non-playing captain)
Ryder Cup Wins: 1979, 1981, 1983, tie 1989, 1993
Major Wins: 1 (U.S. Open 1992)

Leonard

Whilst not quite fulfilling the potential his early success suggested, Justin Leonard is certainly one of his country's best golfers of the past 20 years.

The talented Texan showed his promise at an early age, winning the 1992 US Amateur Championship and then the Haskins Award in 1994 as the most outstanding collegiate golfer. The same year, Leonard became only the fourth golfer, after Gary Hallberg, Scott Verplank and Phil Mickelson, to go directly from college to the PGA Tour without going through Q School.

Leonard had already won two PGA events before 1997, which then became his best year to date. He had started the major calendar in fine form, finishing joint seventh at the Masters. But it was at The Open at Troon that he wrote his name into golfing folklore, producing one of the greatest comebacks in major history.

Leonard started the final round five shots adrift of leader Jesper Parnevik, but he raced to the turn in just 31 strokes and drew level at the 16th with another birdie. Another followed at the par three 17th, where he holed an incredible 30-foot putt to put himself in the lead. There was no way back for the Swede, and Leonard held his nerve to win by three strokes.

The Texan wasn't finished there, finishing second in the season's final major, the PGA Championship. Leonard was tied with compatriot Davis Love III after three rounds, but Love shot an incredible final round 66 to win by five shots.

The following year, Leonard bagged the prestigious Players Championship and nearly won another Open Championship in 1999, narrowly losing a playoff to Paul Lawrie at Carnoustie.

However, later in 1999 Leonard became the focus of arguably the most infamous incident in golf history. The Ryder Cup in Brookline was Leonard's second appearance in the event after he had been on the losing side at Valderrama two years previously, and Europe raced

into a seemingly unassailable 10-6 lead come the final day's singles.

But spurred on by a rallying cry from captain Ben Crenshaw, the U.S. team began to claw their way back. Three matches were still out on the course, when, on the 17th green, Leonard holed a remarkable 45-foot birdie, and began to run around in a frenzy, punching the air in delight. He was soon swamped by caddies, team-mates and the players' wives.

However, José María Olazábal still had a birdie putt of his own that, if holed, would leave him one up going to the 18th. With his concentration broken, he missed. On the BBC's Letter from America Alistair Cooke called the green invasion 'the arrival of the golf hooligan'.

Leonard made his return to the Ryder Cup in Valhalla in 2008, nine years after he helped secure America's last victory in the event. Finding the perfect foil in partner Hunter Mahan, he was in excellent form all weekend, putting two and a half vital points on the board and helping his team romp home. The cup was back on American soil and Leonard's final appearance meant he could finally bow out in style.

Name: Justin Charles Garrett Leonard
Born June 15th 1972, Texas, USA
Ryder Cups: 1997, 1999, 2008
Ryder Cup Wins: 1999, 2008
Major Wins: 1 (The Open Championship 1997)

Littler

Right: *Gene Littler*

Gene Littler won the California State Amateur and U.S. Amateur Championships in 1953 and he was then selected for the Walker Cup. The following year he won a PGA Tour event, the San Diego Open, while still an amateur. He then served briefly in the U.S. Navy before turning professional in 1954. Later that summer he announced himself on the world stage by finishing second (by a single shot) to Ed Furgol at the U.S. Open.

After four tour victories the following year, he decided to adjust his swing but he then suffered a drop in form. It wasn't until 1959 that he was back to his best, taking five tour victories and earning selection for the 1961 Ryder Cup. In the run-up to the event he won the U.S. Open, a final round 68 ensuring he overhauled Doug Sanders and Bob Goalby. He also lost a playoff against old friend and great rival Billy Casper at the 1970 Masters.

With an overall record of 14 wins, five losses and eight halves from 27 Ryder Cup matches, he remains one of the standout players in team America history. Soon after the 1971 Ryder Cup, Littler was diagnosed with malignant melanoma but he recovered to win five events on the 1972 tour. In recognition of his fight-back from illness he received first the 1973 Ben Hogan Award and then the Bob Jones Award, the United States Golf Association's highest honour.

In 1977 he took part in the first sudden-death playoff at a major, but he lost the PGA Championship to Lanny Wadkins. Littler played on the Senior Tour for another 20 years and was inducted into the World Golf Hall of Fame in 1990.

Name: Gene Alec Littler
Born: July 21st 1930, California, USA
Ryder Cups: 1961, 1963, 1965, 1967, 1969, 1971, 1975
Ryder Cup Wins: 1961, 1963, 1965, 1967, tie 1969, 1971, 1975
Major Wins: 1 (U.S. Open 1961)

Love

Davis Love followed in his father's footsteps (he was a former professional golfer and well-known instructor). While at the University of North Carolina, Love became a three-time all-Atlantic Coast Conference (ACC) and all-American golfer. During his student years he also won six amateur titles, including the 1984 ACC tournament championship.

He turned professional in 1985 and was then listed in the top 10 of the Official World Golf Rankings for more than nine years, climbing to number three at his peak. He won his first tournament at the MCI Heritage Golf Classic in 1987. He has since won another 35 professional titles, including 20 on the PGA Tour. Love's one major win came at the 1997 PGA Championship. He has also managed two second-place finishes at the Masters, in 1995 and 1999, second again at the U.S. Open in 1996, and a fourth-place finish at The Open Championship in 2003.

Love's first Ryder Cup was the narrow American victory at The Belfry in 1993 – he secured the vital point by beating Constantino Rocca at the 18th. Thereafter, aside from the controversial win at Brookline in 1999, Love only contributed seven points over the next four events as the Americans struggled against strong European sides. He then captained the 2012 team to the brink of victory, only for the Europeans to overturn a four-point deficit on the final day's singles and win by the narrowest of margins. For a player of his talent, his overall Ryder Cup record is surprisingly poor.

Love established a golf course design company in 1994. He has also written a book recalling his father's lessons on life and golf: *Every Shot I Take*. Published in 1997, it won the United States Golf Association's International Book Award the same year.

Above: *Davis Love with his trusty putter*

Name: Davis Milton Love III
Born: April 13th 1964, North Carolina, USA
Ryder Cups: 1993, 1995, 1997, 1999, 2002, 2004, 2012 (as non-playing captain)
Ryder Cup Wins: 1993, 1999
Major Wins: 1 (U.S. PGA 1997)

Mickelson

Phil Mickelson plays left-handed even though he is naturally right-handed. He developed his swing as a youngster by mirroring his father but the unusual tactic worked and he won a golf scholarship to Arizona State University after high school. While still a student, he developed into an outstanding amateur and won three individual NCAA (National Collegiate Athletic Association) championships and three Haskins Awards. In 1990 he also won the U.S. Amateur title, becoming the first left-handed golfer to do so. The following year he became only the fourth golfer in the history of the PGA to win a tour event as an amateur (the Northern Telecom Open).

Mickelson graduated and turned professional in 1992, and he continued with his PGA Tour tournament successes. He has now won 51 professional events, 42 of which were on the PGA Tour. Up until 2004, however, he was labelled the best golfer never to win a major (an 'accolade' now usually bestowed on Colin Montgomerie, Lee Westwood or Ian Poulter) but he finally broke his duck with victory at the 2004 Masters. He followed it up with a second major title at the PGA Championship the following year. He then won his third major and second Masters title in 2006. His most recent major success came at the 2013 Open Championship.

For a player of such skill, his Ryder Cup record, like that of so many wonderful American players of recent times, is uncharacteristically poor. He was unbeaten in 1995 (scoring three points) but Europe rallied superbly in the singles and edged home by a point overall. Another two points in 1997 should have been enough to tie the match but Montgomerie secured a half at the last against Scott Hoch and Europe again took the trophy. His four points at Brookline in 1999 ensured the U.S. finally claimed the Ryder Cup but the entire event was overshadowed by the poor behaviour of the home players and fans.

The Europeans were too strong at

The Belfry in 2002, and then captain Hal Sutton inexplicably chose to pair Mickelson and Woods at Oakland Hills in 2004. As the men barely spoke and the bitter atmosphere between them was palpable, it came as no surprise as first Montgomerie and Harrington and then Clarke and Westwood put them to the sword. Sutton realised his mistake and split them for the four-balls and foursomes but the damage was done and Europe held an unassailable lead going into the singles.

Mickelson had an awful 2006 Ryder Cup and only managed half a point. The Europeans simply blew his side away and won by nine points. Mickelson chipped in with two points in 2008 as this time Faldo's tactics backfired and handed the cup to the Americans. He then had another awful tournament at the K Club and only managed a single win on the Monday, the first day having been washed out by the weather.

The 2012 event at Medinah saw the Americans take a commanding lead into the singles, with Mickelson himself playing beautifully and landing three points. But his opponent on the Sunday, Justin Rose, somehow kept in touch and then landed three monster putts to condemn Mickelson to an improbable defeat. With their best player beaten, European chests puffed out and they eventually won by a single point when Woods missed a putt and conceded.

Name: Philip Alfred Mickelson
Born: June 16th 1970, San Diego, USA
Ryder Cups: 1995, 1997, 1999, 2002, 2004, 2006, 2008, 2010, 2012
Ryder Cup Wins: 1999, 2008
Major Wins: 5 (Masters 2004, 2006, 2010; U.S. PGA 2005; The Open Championship 2013)

Nelson

Larry Nelson's golfing story is a fascinating one. Considering he didn't pick up a club until he was 21, his record as a player is nothing short of phenomenal.

It wasn't until after he left the army in 1968, following an 18-month tour of service in Vietnam, that Nelson swung a club with intent. He then enrolled at college and filled his spare time playing golf.

Within months he was shooting under 70. Nelson and his wife then moved to Florida so he could focus on his game fulltime, and after going through the PGA Tour Qualifying school in 1973 he began playing on the tour itself only four years after taking up the game.

Nelson's breakthrough year was 1979, when he won twice and finished second on the money list to Tom Watson. Two years later, he won his first major, the PGA Championship at The Atlantic Athletic Club by four strokes over one of his Ryder Cup team-mates, Fuzzy Zoeller.

In 1983 he won his second major, the U.S. Open, at one of the toughest championship courses in the world, Oakmont Country Club just outside Pittsburgh. Nelson's form at Oakmont was so impressive that he posted a U.S. Open record score of 65 and 67 over the last 36 holes, breaking a 51-year mark established by Gene Sarazen.

Finally, in 1987, he won his final major and second PGA Championship at Florida's PGA National Golf Club at Palm Beach Gardens, although he had to overcome his Ryder Cup partner Lanny Wadkins in a playoff.

Yet it is for his performances in the Ryder Cup that Nelson deserves credit. Indeed no American has achieved more in the event. He remains the only player to win five out of five at a single event, in which five was the maximum a player could play. Alongside partner Lanny Wadkins, Nelson won all four of his foursomes and four-ball matches before going on to beat Seve Ballesteros in the singles. And he wasn't finished

there. Two years later, he notched up another 100 per cent record, winning all four of his matches to post a staggering nine points out of nine in his first two Ryder Cups.

Many believe that the 1981 team was the best to have ever played in the Ryder Cup. With the likes of Nicklaus (playing his final Ryder Cup), Watson, Trevino, Floyd and Kite, Dave Marr's 'Untouchables' were simply irresistible in their record 18½-9½ dismantling of John Jacobs's team.

Nelson went on to play in one more event, the 1987 loss at Ohio's Muirfield Village, where his perfect record finally fell. He never won another major but he did enjoy a successful Champions Tour career (19 wins) before being elected to the World Golf Hall of Fame in April 2006.

Name: Larry Gene Nelson
Born: September 10th 1947, Alabama, USA
Ryder Cups: 1979, 1981, 1989
Ryder Cup Wins: 1979, 1983, tie 1989
Major Wins: 3 (U.S. PGA 1981, 1987; U.S. Open 1983)

Nicklaus

Opposite: *Jack Nicklaus plays out of a bunker*

Known as The Golden Bear, Jack Nicklaus was undoubtedly the finest golfer in the game's history. He played professionally from 1961 until his emotional retirement at St. Andrews in 2005, where he received a 10-minute standing ovation from the crowd on the 18th while he waited on the iconic Swilcan Bridge. He then knocked in a 15-foot birdie putt as if to remind the world of golf what it would be missing.

Nicklaus started playing when he was 10, and by 12 he had won the first of five straight Ohio State Junior titles. He won another 26 amateur titles throughout the 1950s and then took the 1959 U.S. Amateur Championships. He then made a serious impression at the 1960 U.S. Open, where he finished second to great rival Arnold Palmer, before winning the U.S. Amateur Championships for the second time in 1961. He turned professional at the end of the year.

His professional debut at the 1962 U.S. Open became his first major championship victory. The following year he won the Masters and the PGA Championship. He then won the Open Championship in 1966 for the first time, and the Masters for the second time. Nicklaus not only became the first golfer to win the Masters two years in a row, but by the age of 26 he'd become the youngest golfer to have won all four major championships. Nicklaus went on to win another 10 majors between 1970 and 1980 and he also became the first player to achieve double and triple slams of the four major championships.

Throughout his professional career Nicklaus racked up 115 wins, including 73 on the PGA Tour. From the McCormack's World Golf Rankings' inception in 1968, Nicklaus was ranked number one every year until 1977. His final major, the 1986 Masters, was won at the age of 46, which remains a record. He also set a record by being the only golfer to finish in the top 10 in every championship for 24 consecutive seasons (1960-1983).

He competed at the Ryder Cup six

times and captained the team twice, winning five as a player and once as captain. He will be best remembered for two moments at the event that came to define him: the legendary concession at Royal Birkdale in 1969 and the push to have European players included in the Great Britain & Ireland side to make the match more competitive.

The 1969 Ryder Cup was Nicklaus's first despite the fact that he was 29 (eligibility rules had excluded him from previous events). The tournament had been marred by poor sportsmanship from both sets of players but it eventually came down to the final singles match between Nicklaus and Tony Jacklin. Jacklin was one down after 16 but he holed an incredible eagle putt on 17 to square the match. Nicklaus then made a tricky five-footer on the 18th before conceding a pressure putt from a couple of feet. Both their match and the Ryder Cup were shared, although the Americans retained the trophy. Nicklaus's gesture was seen by some of his own players as verging on

Above: *Jack Nicklaus of the USA waves to the crowd as he stands on the Swilcan bridge*

the criminal but by the wider world as one of the greatest acts of sportsmanship not just in golf but in all of sport. The atmosphere between the camps was uneasy and Nicklaus knew he could take the edge off things by not forcing Jacklin to play his last shot. His captain, Sam Snead, suggested afterwards that it was the greatest golf match ever played.

The Americans had dominated the post-war Ryder Cup and had won 18 of the next 22 events. It was so one-sided that several Americans refused to play and the event was in danger of becoming a sideshow without a long-term future. The decision to include Europeans was taken when Jack Nicklaus approached the Earl of Derby, who was President of the Professional Golfers' Association, in 1977. The Europeans were thumped 17-11 in West Virginia and then trounced again two years later at Walton Heath when the Americans brought arguably the greatest Ryder Cup side ever assembled across the Atlantic.

It was becoming apparent that the decision to bring in the Europeans was backfiring. To save the event from being cancelled, the European PGA asked Tony Jacklin, one of Britain's most successful players, to lead the next side, to which he agreed, but only if the infrastructure, training facilities and amenities were all of the highest standard (as they were in America). This finally marked the turning point when the Europeans became competitive.

The impact of Nicklaus's intervention can still be felt today: the European team is no longer the weaker side and such is the interest in the Ryder Cup that it has now mushroomed into one of the great global sporting events.

Off the golf course, Nicklaus has published books ranging from instruction manuals to biographies. He also manages one of the world's largest golf course design companies and runs his own event on the PGA Tour, the Memorial Tournament.

Name: Jack William Nicklaus
Born: January 21st 1940, Columbus, Ohio, USA
Ryder Cups: 1969, 1971, 1973, 1975, 1977, 1981 and as non-playing captain: 1983, 1987
Ryder Cup Wins: tie 1969, 1971, 1973, 1975, 1977, 1981, 1983 (as non-playing captain)
Major Wins: 18 (Masters 1963, 1965, 1966, 1972, 1975, 1986; U.S Open 1962, 1967, 1972, 1980; The Open Championship 1966, 1970, 1978; U.S PGA 1963, 1971, 1973, 1975, 1980)

O'Meara

Opposite: *Mark O'Meara practising alongside his great friend Tiger Woods*

One of the most popular American golfers of the modern era, Mark O'Meara took up the game after his family moved onto a Californian golf course when he was 13. He was good enough to earn a scholarship to Long Beach State University, and his collegiate career peaked when he defeated John Cook in the finals of the 1979 U.S. Amateur Championship. O'Meara turned professional in 1980, and joined the PGA Tour the following year.

An accomplished golfer throughout his career, O'Meara secured his first PGA Tour win in 1984 in the Greater Milwaukee Open. Another two victories came in 1985, including the Pebble Beach National Pro-Am, a tournament O'Meara would go on to win a record five times. However, for many years, he never truly threatened to snare one of the game's biggest prizes. And then in 1998 he produced one of the most incredible seasons golf has ever known.

During a heady three-month period, O'Meara blossomed into a two-time major winner. Partly inspired by Tiger Woods, with whom he had become friends, O'Meara first won the Masters. His victory, which came at the 15th attempt (still a record), was secured with a birdie on the final hole to win by one stroke over compatriots David Duval and Fred Couples.

Three months later at Royal Birkdale, O'Meara won a playoff against Brian Watts to win the tournament he coveted more than any other. "This to me is the greatest championship, and I feel fortunate to have my name on the claret jug," said O'Meara. "No disrespect to the others, because the Masters, U.S. Open and PGA are fine championships, but this is the way golf should be played."

He finished his remarkable year by winning the Cisco World Match Play Championship and reached a career best of second in the Official World Golf Rankings.

Before his annus mirabilis, O'Meara had represented the United States in four Ryder Cups, winning one and tying another. His finest individual performance came in 1991's highly charged 'War on the Shore' at Kiawah Island, where he helped inspire America to a memorable one-point victory. Alongside Paul Azinger, his 7&6 win against Nick Faldo and David Gilford remains the joint highest margin of victory in a foursomes match.

His sterling 1998 performances ensured he would be part of the 1999 American team and have one final shot at golf's greatest team event. Despite a poor individual performance, which saw O'Meara lose both of his matches, America fought back on the final day to beat Europe by a solitary point and record one of the game's greatest comebacks.

Name: Mark Francis O'Meara
Born: January 13th 1957, North Carolina, USA
Ryder Cups: 1985, 1989, 1991, 1997, 1999
Ryder Cup Wins: tie 1989, 1991, 1999
Major Wins: 2 (Masters 1998; The Open Championship 1998)

Palmer

Right: *Arnold Palmer of the USA lines up a putt*

Arnold Palmer is regarded as one of the greatest professional golfers in the history of the sport. He was one of the 'Big Three' who, alongside Jack Nicklaus and Gary Player, dragged the sport into the modern, television era and helped popularise it worldwide.

Palmer was initially taught by his father, and he won a golf scholarship to Wake Forest University. He won the U.S. Amateur Championship in 1954 and immediately turned professional.

Palmer won his first major championship at the 1958 Masters and was then credited with cementing the status of The Open Championship among American golfers who had previously viewed the tournament as insignificant because of the lower prize money and long travel time. Palmer knew that to join the game's elite alongside Bobby Jones, Ben Hogan, Walter Hagen and Sam Snead, the claret jug had to be in your trophy cabinet, and it would also raise his profile around the world. Having already won The Masters and U.S. Open in 1960,

he went to St. Andrews in the hope of emulating the incredible Hogan Slam of 1953. He fell agonisingly short, losing to Kel Nagle by a shot, but the British public and American players had both taken note. Palmer returned in 1961 and 1962 to claim the elusive claret jug.

Overall he won 95 professional titles, including 62 PGA Tour and

six Ryder Cups but the contest was so one-sided at the time that he was never on the losing team. He then captained the team to victory in 1975, precipitating the change to include European players in the British side. This change, carried through by his great rival Jack Nicklaus, revitalised the event and eventually led to the extraordinary standard of golf we see today.

The King was inducted into the World Golf Hall of Fame in 1974, and, in 1998, he received the PGA Tour Lifetime Achievement Award.

10 Champions' Tour events, with 29 victories between 1960 and 1963 alone. His charisma, affability, good looks, and penchant for taking on impossible shots to please the crowds meant that television companies returned to the sport en masse and he became something of a golfing ambassador and global icon.

Between 1961 and 1973 he played in

Name: Arnold Daniel Palmer
Born: September 10th 1929, Pennsylvania, USA
Ryder Cups: 1961, 1963, 1965, 1967, 1971, 1973, 1975 (as non-playing captain)
Ryder Cup Wins: 1961, 1963 (as playing captain), 1965, 1967, 1971, 1973, 1975 (as non-playing captain)
Major Wins: 7 (Masters 1958, 1960, 1962, 1964; U.S. Open 1960; The Open Championship 1961, 1962)

Sarazen

Eugenio Saraceni began caddying aged 10 before teaching himself to play the sport. By his mid-teens he'd developed the interlocking grip and was an accomplished club pro. He then won his first major at the 1922 U.S. Open. Long before Nicklaus, Palmer and Player became the 'Big Three', Sarazen, Bobby Jones and Walter Hagen dominated golf globally and helped make the United States the sport's superpower.

Sarazen is credited with inventing the sand wedge, which he developed in secret and then used at the 1932 Open, which he promptly won. He then became the first player to win all four majors, although for much of his early career he was still overshadowed by Walter Hagen.

Sarazen is perhaps best remembered for some incredible single shots, most notably 'the shot that was heard around the world' at the 1935 Masters. On the 15th hole of his final round he was left with 235 yards to the green but he was three shots behind leader Craig Wood (to whom the winner's cheque had already been written) and had a poor lie. He was still considering the shot when playing partner Hagen joked that he'd like to finish in time to meet his date that evening.

Sarazen played perhaps the finest four-wood in history and holed out for an albatross. This tied him with Wood after 72 holes and he then won the playoff the next day. The Sarazen Bridge at Augusta commemorates this incredible strike. He unleashed another remarkable shot at the 1923 U.S. Open during a playoff against Hagen. At the second extra hole, Sarazen hit into the woods but his ball bounced off the roof of a hut and remained in bounds. Sarazen blasted his second through the trees to within three feet, pressurising Hagen into missing an easy putt and surrendering championship. His third shot came at the 1973 Open at Troon when he holed in one at the age of 71.

Sarazen played in six Ryder Cups

and won four in what was a period of American dominance. He secured points at every tournament and remained unbeaten in all 12 matches, a remarkable record for this supremely talented golfer.

In 1997, one month before his death at the age of 97, he drove off The Masters, a fitting end to the career of one of the sport's legends.

Name: Gene Sarazen
Born: February 27th 1902, New York, USA
Died: May 13th 1999, Florida, USA
Ryder Cups: 1927, 1929, 1931, 1933, 1935, 1937
Ryder Cup Wins: 1927, 1931, 1935, 1937
Major Wins: 7 (Masters 1935; U.S. Open 1922, 1932; U.S. PGA 1922, 1923, 1933; The Open Championship 1932)

Above: *A crowd gathers to watch American Gene Sarazen at the Ryder Cup in Leeds.*

Snead

Right: *Sam Snead*

Like many early American professionals Sam Snead came from an impoverished background (later in his career he became known as 'the affluent hillbilly'). Snead was another golfer in the Sarazen mould who was self-taught and started playing with homemade clubs. He joined the professional circuit in 1934 and joined the PGA Tour two years later.

He eventually won the Greensboro Open eight times, a record for single tournament not matched until Tiger Woods won his eighth Arnold Palmer Invitational in 2013. Today he still holds the record for the most wins on the PGA Tour with 82 (out of a total of 165 professional titles).

It took longer for Snead to progress to winning majors, his first being the U.S. PGA in 1942. His career was interrupted by the war but his best results came between 1946 and 1954 when he won three more majors and also came second three times at the U.S. Open, a tournament he was destined never to win.

Even though the post-war American team was considerably stronger than the British side, his record at the Ryder Cup is unsurpassed: eight tournaments as either player or captain or both, with seven wins and the famous 'concession' tie in 1969. He was an exceptional driver

(in a 2000 poll), he still holds records for the oldest player to make the cut at a major (67), oldest player to win a PGA Tour event (52), first player to win PGA events in four separate decades, first player to finish in the top 20 of a major in five different decades (since matched by Tom Watson), the first player to win a pro tournament in six different decades, and the first PGA player to shoot his age (67 at the 1979 Quad Cities Open).

Name: Samuel Jackson Snead
Born: May 27th 1912, Virginia, USA
Died: May 23rd 2002, Virginia
Ryder Cups: 1937, 1947, 1949, 1951 (as playing captain), 1953, 1955, 1959 (as playing captain), 1969 (as non-playing captain)
Ryder Cup Wins: 1937, 1947, 1949, 1951 (as playing captain), 1953, 1955, 1959 (as playing captain), tie 1969 (as non-playing captain)
Major Wins: 7 (Masters 1949, 1952, 1954; The Open Championship 1946; U.S. PGA 1942, 1949, 1951)

into the wind and was precise with both long and short irons. Like Seve in the 1970s and 1980s, he helped pioneer outrageous sand-iron shots from heavy rough, as well as experimenting with stances and grips.

Voted the third best player of all time

Stewart

Right: *Payne Stewart of the United States in action*

Payne Stewart first played on the Asian Tour because he hadn't yet earned a PGA Tour card. By 1982 he had qualified for the tour and he promptly won his first event, the Quad Cities Open. He went on to win 11 PGA Tour events and 24 overall, and was ranked in the world's top 10 for 250 weeks between 1986 and 1993.

Stewart's three major championships were at the U.S. Open in 1991 and 1999, and the PGA Championship in 1989. In the latter, he was six shots behind Mike Reid as the pair began the final round. With holes running out, Stewart made up five shots on 16, 17 and 18 to take an improbable victory. (He rallied from a similar position against Scott Simpson at the 1991 U.S. Open when he was two shots behind with three to play in the playoff, although he then blew Simpson away to win by two shots.) He sealed his last major with a 15-foot putt at Pinehurst that condemned Mickelson, Woods and Singh to the minor places after an epic final round.

As well as playing for the United States on three World Cup teams, Stewart also represented his country five times at the Ryder Cup, although his comment in 1999 that the Europeans should only be caddying for his side was somewhat uncharacteristic. A fervent supporter

tragic end in 1999 only months after his third major. The plane he was travelling in suffered a gradual loss of cabin pressure and crashed. Aged only 42, and with much of his career still ahead of him, Stewart and five others were killed, including his agents Robert Fraley and Van Ardan, and Bruce Borland, one of Jack Nicklaus's architects from his golf course design company.

Stewart was inducted into the World Golf Hall of Fame in 2001. The PGA Tour introduced the Payne Stewart Award in 2000, and the Payne Stewart Golf Club was opened in Missouri in 2009.

of the tournament, he realised he had overstepped the mark and graciously conceded defeat to Colin Montgomerie in their singles match because of the awful abuse being hurled at the Scotsman by the American fans.

Stewart's colourful career came to a

Name: William Payne Stewart
Born: January 30th 1957, Missouri, USA
Died: October 25th 1999, Florida, USA
Ryder Cups: 1987, 1989, 1991, 1993, 1999
Ryder Cup Wins: tie 1989, 1991, 1993, 1999
Major Wins: 3 (U.S. PGA 1989; U.S. Open 1991, 1999)

Strange

A self-contained, intensely competitive and highly professional man, Curtis Strange is famed for a career that promised to rank alongside that of the greats but eventually fell just short. One moment he was the brightest star in the golfing world, the next he simply stopped winning. During his brief peak, however, he was one of the best golfers of the 1980s.

Strange came from a golfing family. Before his untimely death at only 38, his dad Tom was a club professional, and Curtis and his twin brother Allan both started playing aged just seven. His first title was the Virginia Junior Championship, and he then earned the Arnold Palmer Scholarship to play golf at Wake Forest University. It was here that he was a member of the NCAA Championship team with Jay Haas and Bob Byman that Golf World labelled 'the greatest of all time'.

Strange's emergence on the tour came as the era of Nicklaus and Watson drew to a close, but the search for an American superstar to rank alongside the greats

of the past initially drew a blank. Enter Strange.

At Augusta in 1985, he had one arm in the green jacket but he then capitulated on the last six holes, eventually finishing two shots behind Bernhard Langer. Such a gut-wrenching defeat would have crushed most players but not Strange. He slowly regained the confidence and mentality needed to secure the biggest tournaments, and come the 1988 U.S. Open at Brookline, he was ready to shake off the reputation as the best player to have never won a major.

Holding off a spirited challenge from Nick Faldo, Strange triumphed after an 18-hole playoff to win his first major, a title he memorably defended at Oak Hill the following year. With this, he became only the second man after the great Ben Hogan to win back-to-back U.S. Opens.

It was during this time that he played in four memorable Ryder Cups (his fifth and final competition was in 1995). Overall, his Ryder Cup record is not as impressive as it should have been,

Left: *Curtis Strange*

however: Strange played in 20 matches, winning six, halving two and losing 12, giving him a return of only seven points. He only played in one winning team, in 1983 at The Belfry.

In 2002, Strange succeeded Ben Crenshaw as captain of the American Ryder Cup team at The Belfry. Strange's side performed admirably but the cup ended up in European hands after an emphatic performance in the singles.

An emotional Strange conceded the best team had won. "We always like to win but it's a great atmosphere to be a part of."

Name: Curtis Northrup Strange
Born: January 30th 1955, Virginia, USA
Ryder Cups: 1983, 1985, 1987, 1989, 1995, 2002 (as non-playing captain)
Ryder Cup Wins: 1983, tie 1989
Major wins: 2 (U.S. Open 1988, 1989)

Trevino

Lee Trevino left school at 14 to work as a caddy and shoe shiner. His uncle then gave him a few balls and an old club so he used his spare time to practise. He then served for four years in the United States Marine Corps. When he left, he became club pro in El Paso but he didn't join the PGA Tour until 1967, a year in which he came fifth at the U.S. Open behind illustrious names like Nicklaus and Palmer.

He continued improving and won the tournament in 1968 before taking the first of his two Open Championships in 1971. This was a tremendous period in his career as in just three weeks he won The Open, U.S. Open and Canadian Open. He also won the PGA championship in 1974 and 1984, taking his career tally to 89 professional wins, of which 29 came on the PGA Tour.

Trevino also played for the Ryder Cup team six times and was captain in 1985. This was an era of American dominance, however, and he never lost as a player. After his fourth win at the event he was struck by lightning while playing in Chicago. He had surgery to correct the resulting spinal injuries and managed to recover to reach number two in the world rankings. He later joked that he would only ever play golf again with a one-iron as "not even God can hit a one-iron".

After Jack Nicklaus's intervention, the British Ryder Cup side allowed European golfers into the fold for the first time and they soon became a different prospect. With Trevino as captain in 1985, the Americans were expected to continue their dominance but Tony Jacklin had rebuilt the European side and they had finally become a professional outfit with the backroom staff to match. Trevino tasted defeat for the first time in his Ryder Cup career as Jacklin masterminded a five-point win at The Belfry.

Throughout his career, Trevino was known for his practical jokes and quips to the press. Before a playoff with Jack Nicklaus at the 1971 U.S. Open, he threw a rubber snake at his opponent. His humour even landed him a cameo

Above: *Lee Trevino hits left handed over the ditch*

role in the 1996 comedy *Happy Gilmore*. But he was a curious character who boycotted The Masters because he felt the establishment was elitist and the course didn't suit his fade style of play. He later regretted his decision and returned to play at Augusta, but by then he wasn't competitive and never won the fourth major.

Trevino was PGA Player of the Year in 1971, won the Vardon Trophy five times between 1970 and 1980, and was inducted into the World Golf Hall of Fame in 1981.

Name: Lee Buck Trevino
Born: December 1st 1939, Dallas, USA
Ryder Cups: 1969, 1971, 1973, 1975, 1979, 1981, 1985 (as non-playing captain)
Ryder Cup Wins: tie 1969, 1971, 1973, 1975, 1979, 1981
Major Wins: 6 (U.S. Open 1968, 1971; The Open Championship 1971, 1972; U.S. PGA 1974, 1984)

Wadkins

When asked about the most successful American Ryder Cup golfers of all time, most people respond with the usual names: Snead, Watson, Nicklaus and Palmer. Yet, when it comes to team golf's biggest event, Lanny Wadkins's record is up there with the best. He compiled 21½ points from his nine appearances and his never-say-die attitude was a major reason why he enjoyed such success in the competition.

Wadkins turned professional in 1971, the year after he had won the U.S. Amateur Championship by one stroke from Tom Kite. He didn't have to wait long for his first PGA Tour victory, the 1972 Sahara Invitational in Las Vegas, where he finished one stroke ahead of Arnold Palmer, his university scholarship benefactor.

However, his form dipped shortly afterwards and for three years it looked as if Wadkins would never escape the rut. But in 1977 at the PGA Championship at Pebble Beach, he bounced back in spectacular fashion, winning the only major title of his career in a sudden-death playoff against Gene Littler, the first time the sudden-death format was used in a stroke-play major championship.

Wadkins went on to finish runner-up in four more majors (the U.S. Open in 1986, and the PGA Championship in 1982, 1984 and 1987). In the twilight of his career, his game finally took a shine to Augusta, and he posted three third-place finishes in a four-year period (1990, 1991 and 1993).

But it was with his sole major victory in 1977 that Wadkins paved the way for his remarkable Ryder Cup journey, a love affair with the event that would span three decades. He finished on the winning team on his first three appearances until Europe's resurgence under Tony Jacklin in the mid-1980s.

His most memorable early appearance came in 1983 when he held his nerve and essentially won the United States the match. After the disappointments of the next two tournaments, both Wadkins and the American side bounced back in

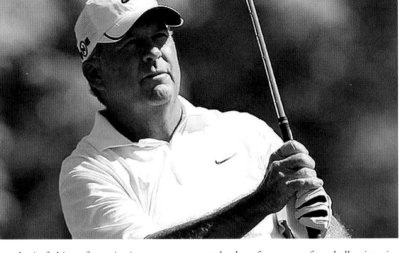

emphatic fashion, first winning a narrow contest at Kiawah Island in 1991, and then retaining the trophy with another one-point victory at The Belfry in 1993.

Two years later, at Oak Hill, Wadkins took part in his final Ryder Cup, this time as captain. However, the Europeans were determined to regain the trophy and despite trailing by two points going into the singles, it was their turn to emerge victorious by a solitary point, securing the first and only win under Bernard Gallacher's rein.

Despite Wadkins's loss in his final Ryder Cup, his record is outstanding, especially when paired up. He jointly holds the record for most foursome matches won (nine) with Arnold Palmer

and also for most four-ball victories (seven), also with Palmer.

When it comes to most matches won overall, Wadkins is in joint second place alongside Billy Casper on 20. Only Arnold Palmer with 22 has won more. Finally, he stands alone in third place on most points won, with a sterling 21½, only two behind all-time leader Billy Casper.

Name: Jeremy Lanston 'Lanny' Wadkins
Born: December 5th 1949, Virginia, USA
Ryder Cups: 1977, 1979, 1983, 1985, 1987, 1989, 1991, 1993, 1995 (as non-playing captain)
Ryder Cup Wins: 1977, 1979, 1983, tie 1989, 1991, 1993
Major Wins: 1 (U.S. PGA 1977)

Watson

Tom Watson started playing golf with his father and he went on to win four Missouri State Amateur Championships from 1968 to 1971. After playing on his university golf team, Watson turned professional and joined the PGA Tour in 1971. He first made an impression at a major at the 1974 U.S. Open and led going into the final round. He faded badly, however, and could only finish fifth.

Byron Nelson recognised his talent and became his mentor/tutor, and only two weeks later Watson won his first tour title at the Western Open. His first major, The Open, followed in 1975. It was a tournament that Watson would eventually win five times and cement his reputation as the finest links golfer of his generation. In 2009, at the age of 59, he made a remarkable and emotional return to the top of the leaderboard at Turnberry. He only needed to make par at the 18th to secure a record-equalling sixth Open (with Harry Vardon) but he missed an eight-foot putt and then lost a playoff to

Stewart Cink. The consensus amongst experts and armchair pundits alike was that had he pulled off the win it would have been the most remarkable achievement in all of sport.

At the same course 32 years earlier, Watson and Nicklaus, already the best players on the planet, became sporting immortals during the 'Duel in the Sun'. After two rounds, they were tied for the lead and were paired together for the third round. They threw everything at each other and both shot 65. Paired again for the final round, they traded birdies and were still level after 16 holes, at which point Watson cast his eyes across the sunburnt galleries and turned to Nicklaus. "This is what it's all about, isn't it?" he said.

"You bet," Nicklaus replied.

Their compelling tussle continued up the 17th, although Nicklaus ceded the advantage to the younger man when he missed his birdie putt and Watson knocked his in. On the 18th Nicklaus drove into the rough while Watson hit the fairway. Nicklaus played an incredible recovery to

40 feet but Watson was only two feet from the pin. Nicklaus then made an incredible birdie, but Watson's birdie gave him victory in the finest tournament played in the latter half of the 20th century. Nicklaus threw an arm around his shoulder and led him off the course in yet another display of sportsmanship.

Watson's career thereafter went from strength to strength and he was world number one for four consecutive years (1978-82). He was also a key figure in three successful American Ryder Cup sides as a player, as well as captaining the victorious 1993 side. He was then chosen to captain the side at Gleneagles in 2014.

Watson was named PGA Player of the Year six times and was inducted into the World Golf Hall of Fame in 1988. In his later career, he won three Senior British Open titles, in 2003, 2005 and 2007, and in 2010 he finished joint 18th at The Masters at Augusta. Although he only finished 22nd at the 2011 Open Championship, he shot a hole-in-one at the sixth and remains one of the most popular players in the sport.

Name: Thomas Sturges Watson
Born: September 4th 1949, Missouri, USA
Ryder Cups: 1977, 1981, 1983, 1989, 1993 (as non-playing captain)
Ryder Cup Wins: 1977, 1981, 1983, tie 1989, 1993 (as non-playing captain)
Major Wins: 8 (Masters 1977, 1981; U.S. Open 1982; The Open Championship 1975, 1977, 1980, 1982, 1983)

Above: *Tom Watson about to win the British Open Golf Championship*

Woods

Tiger Woods started playing golf before he was two years old, and, prior to his third birthday, he won the Under-10 California Drive, Pitch & Putt competition. He went on to win the Junior World Championship six times, with four consecutive wins from 1988 to 1991. By the time he was 20 he had won three consecutive U.S. Amateur titles and the silver medal at The Open Championship as the leading amateur.

Woods left college to turn professional in 1996 and signed two multi-million-dollar endorsement contracts with Nike and Titleist. He won two events in his first year, which meant he qualified for the Tour Championship. In April the following year he won his first major, The Masters, with a record score of 18 under par. He was the first African-American and the youngest player to take the title. Woods's professional career blossomed, although he endured a temporary slump in late 1997 and early 1998 when he adjusted elements of his technique.

Woods has won 14 major championships overall, second only to Jack Nicklaus (18). He is also the only golfer since Nicklaus to have achieved a career triple Grand Slam. Woods has now won 79 PGA Tour events, second only to Sam Snead, although if he can recover from recent back surgery he has much of his career ahead of him and will surely secure the four more titles he needs.

Due to revelations about his private life, Woods took time out from professional golf in late 2009 and only returned for the 2010 Masters and the U.S. Open (he finished both in tied fourth position). Later that year he was rated as the world's highest paid professional athlete with endorsements and tournament earnings worth more than $100 million. His form was erratic, however, and his ranking dropped to 58 in 2011. He then set about rebuilding his career and regained the top spot after victory in the 2013 Arnold Palmer Invitational. He has been the PGA Player of the Year a record 11 times.

For such an extraordinary talent, his Ryder Cup record is ordinary at best.

Left: *Tiger Woods celebrates*

He only managed 1½ points in 1997 and was demolished 4&2 by Constantino Rocca in the singles. He only won one foursomes match in 1999, although another point in the singles helped the U.S. to an ugly win at Brookline. He was more successful at The Belfry in 2002 but he was let down by his team-mates and Europe cruised to victory. Hal Sutton then paired him with Phil Mickelson at Oakland Hills but the decision backfired spectacularly as America were routed by nine points. Woods scored three points two years later but he was one of the only Americans to leave the K Club in Ireland in credit as the team was thumped yet again. He wasn't part of the victorious 2008 side in Valhalla, but his three points in a losing cause at Celtic Manor was overshadowed by a humiliating 6&5 loss to Donald and Westwood in the foursomes. He then only managed ½ a point at Medinah in 2012. A return of one win from seven tournaments can't easily be explained, except perhaps that the U.S. team of late has consisted of too many individuals used to playing for themselves whereas the European side has become much greater than the sum of its parts through inspirational leadership and teamwork.

Name: Eldrick Tont 'Tiger' Woods	
Born: December 30th 1975, California, USA	
Ryder Cups: 1997, 1999, 2002, 2004, 2006, 2010, 2012	
Ryder Cup Wins: 1999	
Major Wins: 14 (Masters 1997, 2001, 2002, 2005; U.S. Open 2000, 2002, 2008; The Open Championship 2000, 2005, 2006; U.S. PGA 1999, 2000, 2006, 2007)	

RYDER CUP PLAYER BY PLAYER

**The pictures in this book were provided
courtesy of the following:**

GETTY IMAGES
101 Bayham Street, London NW1 0AG

WIKICOMMONS
commons.wikimedia.org

Design & Artwork by Scott Giarnese

Published by G2 Entertainment Limited

Publishers: Jules Gammond & Edward Adams

Written by Liam McCann & Andrew O'Brien